To Marge and Charlie Raynor
for helping me to set sail

Exploring Bull Island

Sailing and Walking around a
South Carolina Sea Island

Bob Raynor

THE
History
PRESS

Published by The History Press
Charleston, SC 29403
www.historypress.net

Cover Picture:
Snowy and great egrets in Jacks Creek. *Courtesy of Brad Floyd and Coastal Expeditions.*

Front Cover Inset:
Outward bound with marsh and Bull Island in background. *Courtesy of Susan Raynor*

First published 2005
Second printing 2010

Manufactured in the United States

ISBN 978-1-59629-010-5

Library of Congress Cataloging-in-Publication Data

Raynor, Bob.
Exploring Bull Island : sailing and walking around a South Carolina sea
island / Bob Raynor.
p. cm.
Includes bibliographical references and index.
ISBN 978-1-59629-010-5 (alk. paper)
1. Raynor, Bob--Travel--South Carolina--Bull Island. 2. Raynor,
Bob--Diaries. 3. Natural history--South Carolina--Bull Island. 4.
Sailing--South Carolina--Bull Island. 5. Walking--South Carolina--Bull
Island. 6. Bull Island (S.C.)--Description and travel. 7. Bull Island
(S.C.)--History. I. Title.
F277.C4R39 2005
917.57'91--dc22
2005006941

CONTENTS

Acknowledgements   page 9
Notes on Charts and Maps   page 13
Introduction   page 15

February 20   page 19
The birthday pilgrimage † Anderson Creek † Bull Creek † Cape Romain National Wildlife Refuge † Walk out Beach Road † Great horned owl and turkeys † Livestock on island † Gators on the trail † Red wolves † White-tailed deer at landing † Return passage through ferry route † Completion of sail in darkness.

March 19   page 27
A botched take-off and a necessary jury rig † Misty passage through Anderson and Bull Creeks to dock † The Shark Hole † Early morning interaction with refuge staff † Interpretative trail † Geological heritage † Alligator on the dike † A side trip to wildlife-viewing platform † South on Mill Road to beach † A post-Hugo memory at Big Pond † Middens Trail † Native American heritage and middens † A Hurricane Hugo remnant † Return sail.

April 30   page 37
Broken bow handle † Fruitless search for entrance to Jacks Creek † New berth on the Northeast Point † The 1670 encounter of Sewees and Carolina colonists † Into the forest with biting insects † Walk around the Jacks Creek impoundment † The Old Fort † A commemorative marker † The entrance to Jacks Creek † "New" bird † Back at the Boneyard † Recalling a "lost" boat † Loggerhead sighting on the return passage.

May 25   page 47
Running aground on oysters † Tacking to the Northeast Point † Gator in beach pool † CCC and the building of the Jacks Creek impoundment † Erosion † Barrier island migration † The missing lighthouse † Back along the beach † Thunderheads over the mainland † Across the bay with sighting of Bird Island shoal † Entering Venning Creek for return to landing.

June 10   page 57
Remembering a misadventure † Plans for a circumnavigation † Encountering "snowbirds" † Price Creek † Price Inlet dynamics † A story of near tragedy for the Magwood family † Surprise crowd off the inlet † Coasting along to the northeast

† Round the point, and a lunch landing † Memories of an attempted Wrightsville Beach circumnavigation † Out into the inlet for the final rounding † Passage home.

June 14 page 67

Fast passage to the Northeast Point † Negative tide and horseshoe crabs † Closed area for an endangered beach plant † Endangered species and the refuge † Behavior of black-necked stilts † Talking turtle crawls at the Boneyard with CRNWR staff † Loggerhead turtle nesting in the refuge † Return to *Kingfisher* † Change of homeward course † Bird Island shoal † Home through Venning Creek.

July 20 page 77

Ghosting into Venning Creek † Paddling against the tide † Smooth sailing across the bay to the northeast † Search for Marsh Island † Sighting the island and approaching through surf † The activity of a nesting island † Bird migration † Terns † A past oyster factory in the bay † Return via the Venning passage.

August 10 page 85

Heading out to the refuge dock † Windward work up Bull Creek † Sad state of Dominick House † The familiar walk to beach † A beach/dune/shrub and maritime forest system † Grove of live oaks by Dominick House † Thomas Shubrick and live oaking on Bull Island † The sons of Shubrick and their naval careers † A fishing guide and a croaker † Muddy docking at the landing.

August 26 page 97

Send-off by gator † Bird at the masthead † Startled by wood storks † Closer examination of Little Bull's Island † A fine "mooring" on the south end † Walk around the point to the beach † Searching for the beginning of the Mill Road † Labyrinth of passages † Clandestine activities † *Spartina alterniflora* † Sightings of *Island Cat* and a bald eagle in the bay † Mild embarrassment before landing.

September 13 page 107

Isabel at Category 5 far off coast † Busy landing with shrimp baiters † Friend tags along in kayak † Light wind † PVC poles of baiters line the channel † Union invasion of February 1865 † Around the beach and Jacks Creek dike † The challenge to Jacks Creek after Hugo † Whelks in a shallow inlet † Return across the bay † Reminder of Native American paddlers and the great Sewee trading voyage † A hermit crab revealed.

October 12 page 117

Fog and breeze from north † Arrival at refuge dock before second tour with Rudy Mancke † Fruitless search for island graveyard † "Day on Bulls Island with Rudy

Mancke" † Joining up with group at picnic area † Conversation with Rudy on tour † Naturalists visiting the island in the past † Rudy interpreting nature † The trouble with nomenclature † Last stop at the Boneyard † Circuit trip around Jacks Creek on the return † Little wind and no-see-ums back at the dock † *Island Cat* and *Kingfisher* part ways † Glassy bay and no wind † A paddle across Shortcut Shoal † A beat into a light northwest wind † Cloud of no-see-ums at the landing.

November 23 page 127

Paddling out Anderson Creek † American oystercatchers † Paddling across Shortcut Shoal † Wading and pulling *Kingfisher* † A thirsty oysterman † Father and son canoeists at the dock † A short walk to the graveyard † Deciphering the weathered stones † Return to the wildlife-viewing platform † A kingfisher and foxtail squirrel † Return sail with a plethora of cormorants † Sailing in at dusk.

December 22 page 137

A cold winter solstice morning † Paddling out Anderson Creek by a perched kingfisher † A light north wind at the Shark Hole † Missed landing and a mooring at the Northeast Point † A long walk planned on the year's shortest day † Entering the forest † A gathering of birds at Jacks Creek † Turkeys on the trail † Native American winter solstice † Price Inlet after noon and a pause † Return walk via the beach † Pair of shrimpers parallel walk † Remains on the beach † No wind noticed while passing the shallow inlets † Completion of walk † A frantic search for a forgotten hiking stick † Leaving the stick and the island with a light southwest breeze † Last of breeze at sunset landing.

January 18 page 147

Small craft advisory † "New" bamboo hiking stick rigged † Cherokee kingfisher legends † Laceration after launching † Heavy-weather windward work in the Intracoastal Waterway † Memory of a wet winter sail † A Lowcountry shark tale † Tacking through narrow channels † Off the wind and flying into Bull Creek † Survey of live oaks by Dominick House † Gayer Dominick † Reflection on Sewee sea tragedy † Back into maritime forest through wetlands † Sandspurs and snakes † Slavery and Reconstruction on Bull Island † A new path and amazing view † Humble thoughts † Concern about strong winds on the return passage † Letting *Kingfisher* rip across Shortcut Shoal † Joyful sailing through the creek † A "record" passage.

February 22 page 161

Marking the birthday pilgrimage after two aborted sails † Therapy on the water † Beach Creek † Andrew Magwood's invitation to visit Little Bull's Island † Sizing up the landing † A fine dock on Schooner Creek † Exploring the island † Ethel and Clarence Magwood † Remnants of the original Magwood homestead † A bountiful winter garden † The gift of collards † A granite memorial † Junior

Magwood † The Magwoods and commercial fishing † Across the inlet to search Bull Island for another Magwood homestead † Civilization intruding in the creeks † Home for fresh collards.

Epilogue: April 3   page 173

Bibliography   page 179
Index   page 187
About the Author   page 191

Acknowledgements

The creation of this book was far from a solo voyage. Much help was requested and received throughout the process. I drew on both familiar and new resources in researching Bull Island. I will start locally with Cape Romain National Wildlife Refuge (NWR): long-term staff member Larry Davis helped provide information at different junctures in the project and helped fill in some holes at the end. Cape Romain NWR biologist Sarah Dawsey was most helpful in providing data on management activities and surveys in the refuge and fielding questions. SEWEE Association executive director Karen Beshears was helpful in pointing me in the direction of resources. One of those resources, Ed EuDaly of the U.S. Fish and Wildlife Service, shared with me information about the seabeach amaranth project. In general the staff at the Sewee Center were very helpful.

I drew on Dennis Forsythe of The Citadel for his knowledge of ornithology and general bird matters around Bull Island. I turned to Martha Zierden of The Charleston Museum for resources in prehistory and accepted her advice to move ahead with a publishing deadline. Archaeologist Chris Judge of the South Carolina Department of Natural Resources helped me find those resources. These included visits with Keith Derting of the South Carolina Institute of Archaeology and Anthropology to review site files, and U.S. Forest Service archaeologist Bob Morgan, who shared his knowledge and a recent report on the Sewee Shell Ring. Michael Katuna of the Department of Geology and Environmental Geosciences at the

College of Charleston was kind enough to review my account of the island's geological heritage in a timely manner. Historical researcher Sarah Fick shared several helpful nineteenth-century newspaper items on property auctions. An unexpected and most helpful resource for this project was Bud Hill of The Village Museum in McClellanville. I first learned from Bud about the Magwood family's relationship to Bull Island. Bud shared with me all his files on the island and the Magwoods, and I am indebted to him for his generosity.

I am also indebted to several old friends for their assistance. Gill Guerry steered me toward a graphics application for the map drawing and patiently mentored me along my slow learning curve. Julia O'Shea provided the coverage for my duties at the Institute of Psychiatry at MUSC, allowing me to schedule time off for days on the island and in front of the computer. My old neighbor and current McClellanville resident Ginny Prevost agreed to be the first reader of the entire manuscript. She provided helpful criticism and smoothing of the text in a most timely manner. Two other McClellanville residents, Ted and Dale Rosengarten, provided direction and encouragement with the publishing process. Dale also passed the word on about the work-in-progress in casual conversation to Jason Chasteen of The History Press. Jason's enthusiasm for the project stimulated the progress toward a completed manuscript, and his efforts made this venture into the publishing world a remarkably smooth and easy process. Julie Hiester of The History Press did a fine job on the copyediting and facilitated the effort toward the final product.

Special recognition is reserved for three people. Andrew Magwood invited me into his home and shared his intriguing family history, a gift I will never forget. He also allowed me to visit Little Bull's Island in February of 2004. In the eleventh hour of preparations for sending the book to the printers, Brad Floyd of Coastal Expeditions offered his Bull Island photographs to enhance the manuscript. His appreciation and love of the island are apparent in his fine work. My old friend Steve Hoffius again proved indispensable to one of my projects. His early feedback and advice helped to shape the narrative style, and he guided me through the world of publishing. Time and again Steve's knowledge and resourcefulness helped me along.

Finally, I want to thank my family for their overall support of this project. For my children Sara and Eliot, I appreciate the "loan" of

Kingfisher for these voyages but more importantly for their interest and support of my efforts. Sara found several helpful newspaper articles in Greenville, and Eliot and Sara both provided feedback and encouragement on reading drafts of chapters. I am extremely grateful for the constant and unqualified support for this project from my wife Susan. This support included the knowledge of my venturing out alone on the waters throughout the year in many conditions. The photos that Susan shot grace the book's cover and provide significant visual appeal. But overall Susan's unwavering support for my dedication to this project has allowed me to venture into new territories.

Despite all the great help listed above, and much painstaking effort on my part, I take responsibility for any remaining errors and flaws in the text and maps.

Notes on Charts and Maps

The creation of individual charts and maps to accompany each specific sail and walk has been a project in itself. The enhancement of the reader's orientation was in mind in providing these visual aids to follow the courses and paths traveled. The application software Adobe Illustrator CS was utilized for this process.

The bibliography contains a section listing the charts and maps used as references for the book's drawings. It is important to note that the maps presented here are graphic representations that are only approximations of the details and scale of the actual physical places. I discovered at times a discrepancy between the latest charts and maps by NOAA and USGS, and the current reality. A good example is a trail leading to the dike system near one of the shallow inlets on the east shoreline of the island. The trail on the map always appeared longer than my observations, and I concluded that the forces of erosion had reduced the trail's length to perhaps 10 percent of the recorded distance. Similarly the features of the marsh and shoals are constantly changing.

Information is given at the beginning of each chapter on the pertinent conditions of the day. This information is placed on the bottom right corner of each chart. The date is followed by notations of water temperature (Charleston Harbor) and predicted high air temperature. The low tide listed is one calculated for Jacks Creek, meaning the tidal area between the Northeast Point and the Cape Romain NWR dock. The winds listed are the predicted winds for the day. General information is given on the overall weather predicted. This data was gleaned from both the *News and Courier* and the NOAA marine forecast.

The names for many of the places described in the following text have alternate variations from one map to the next, and from one account to another. I have used names like "Mill Road" instead of "Mills Road." Most importantly, the name of the island itself was equivocal between "Bull" and "Bulls." Though I prefer the Native American name (Onisecaw), for this account I have stuck with "Bull Island."

Both the charts and maps use the following graphic symbols.

Legend

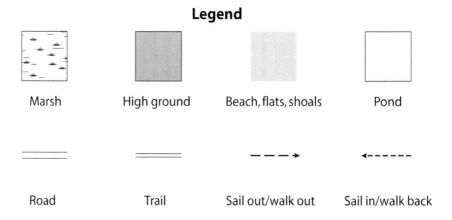

| Marsh | High ground | Beach, flats, shoals | Pond |

| Road | Trail | Sail out/walk out | Sail in/walk back |

Introduction

What we have learned
Is like a handful of earth;
What we have yet to learn
Is like the whole world."
-Avvaiyar

The idea for *Exploring Bull Island: Sailing and Walking Around a South Carolina Sea Island* was conceived in the winter of 2003 after an annual pilgrimage—sailing over to Bull Island around the time of my birthday. Preparation for this project began years ago in my childhood. A photograph at my parents' home in New Jersey shows a young boy sailing a black-hulled craft with a red sail. The boat was a kit-built Sailfish, a wooden precursor of the Sunfish, and in the picture was floating on the waters of the Navesink River, an estuary that connects with Sandy Hook Bay and New York Harbor. The image is a reminder of the development of my love for sailing in those waters. On my infrequent visits to New Jersey I am drawn to the river like a loggerhead turtle to its nesting beach. My sailing skills were honed on more sophisticated sailing craft in very competitive youth racing around the buoys, and these skills provided me employment as a sailing instructor in New Jersey and North Carolina for many summers. Small-boat seamanship has served me well as my interest in racing has waned and my exploration of the natural world has become a passion. My deep abiding love for the coast has drawn me to reside close to the shore, excepting my time in university studies in Chapel Hill, North Carolina.

When I moved to Charleston in December of 1978 to work as a recreation therapist in psychiatry at the Medical University of South Carolina, I brought along my two sailing craft, a Laser and a Hobie 16 catamaran. After marriage, my wife Susan and I looked to put down some roots, and we purchased a three-acre piece of property in Awendaw. I was drawn here by the location—situated along the Intracoastal Waterway directly across from Bull Island and Bulls Bay. Our property is located back in the woods in a fine stand of oak-hickory forest, and I accomplished a dream by constructing my own post-and-beam timber house nestled in these woods. Our community, Romain Retreat, has a landing and dock around three miles from the island, and I made the occasional trip over in the Hobie 16. As our two young children, Sara and Eliot, grew to boating age, they received a gift from their grandparents—a used Sunfish, a class of sailboat that I had utilized as a sailing instructor and appreciated for its youth-friendly qualities. We named the boat *Kingfisher* for the belted kingfishers that we often saw at the neighborhood landing. *Kingfisher* and its winged namesake had similar qualities, such as small size, an unusual rig and character and a distinctive look while in flight. As my children moved on to other interests, I found myself beginning to gravitate toward sailing *Kingfisher* for a number of reasons: lightness, simplicity in rigging and sailing, shallow draft and dependability. Launching this craft solo was easy and I found myself getting out on the water more often. *Kingfisher* was not as fast as my previous boats, but I began to appreciate the sailing qualities as I ventured out in more challenging conditions.

I don't recall my first trip to Bull Island on *Kingfisher*, but sailing over and walking around on the beach became an occasional experience. After my sail and walk in February of 2003, I wrote an account of the trip for friends and family, and at that point the light came on: make one trip a month for the coming year and document my experiences. The idea was soon transformed into a mission, including the exploration and investigation of the natural and cultural history of the island as an integral part of this project. So this simple boat, *Kingfisher*, was transformed into a research vessel allowing me to penetrate the beautiful, complex and mysterious world of creek, marsh, bay and barrier island. Bull Island is not just any barrier island; it has been described as the "crown jewel" of the Cape Romain National Wildlife Refuge. As a destination it is enhanced by its isolation from the mainland with no causeway or bridge to bring automobile traffic to its dirt and sand roads. It is enriched by its natural wonders—verdant maritime forest, extensive freshwater impoundments, beautiful beaches and a wealth of wildlife. Less known to the public is the human history of the island, and my efforts at understanding what happened continued to provoke further questions.

With these matters in mind, I embarked on a twelve-month quest to sail a number of the waterways connecting to the island, walk as many of the roads and trails as possible, and learn extensively about this special place. *Kingfisher* and I joined in a collaborative relationship in exploring this maritime world. Each trip triggered new directions for sails and walks and ideas for inquiry. This search was additionally spurred on by other tantalizing tidbits: the knowledge of colonial bird nesting on an isolated isle in Bulls Bay, a graveyard of former residents on the island and an old photo of a Bull Island lighthouse. I squeezed more than one journey into several months, and not only repeated the birthday pilgrimage but added one more sail in April of 2004 to bring this account to a close. Several sails were flyers off of the main course to small isles that relate to Bull Island. I was aware that there was no book covering the island's history but was clear about not wanting to take on the writing of a comprehensive history. Though this book is not a traditional guide, readers may find the corresponding charts and maps covering each sail and walk of service. Much as *Kingfisher* tacked through the creeks and bay, and I crisscrossed the island on my walks, the narrative weaves through the passages to and from the island, the observations of natural history and the recounting of the people figuring in the legacy of Bull Island.

February 20

N

BULLS BAY

Bird island

Highway 17 North

Doar Road

Charleston 22 miles

Seewee Road

Venning Creek

Romain Retreat

Garris Landing

Intracoastal Waterway

Anderson Creek

N

Sewee Bay

Bull Harbor

Bull Creek

Summerhouse Creek

Northeast Pt.

Jacks Creek

BULL ISLAND

Price Creek

Price Inlet

pers Island

February 20, 2003
Water: 53 Air: 66
Low tide: 4:20 PM
Winds: NE 12–15 knots
Outlook: Time of sun and clouds

0   1   2

Scale in miles

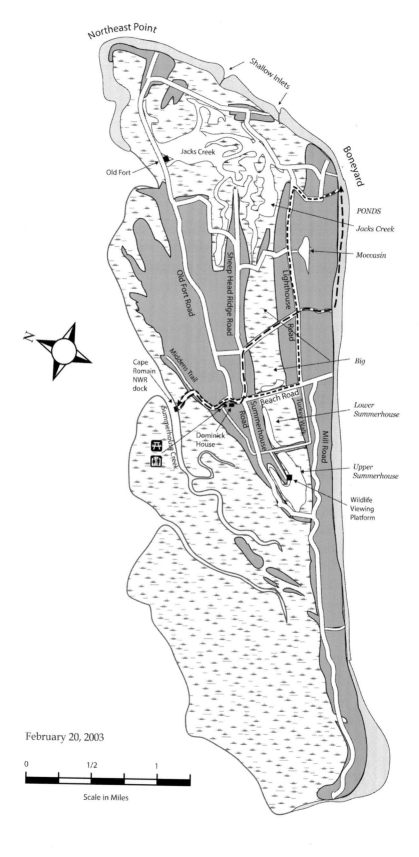

Northeast Point

Shallow Inlets

Boneyard

Jacks Creek

Old Fort

PONDS

Jacks Creek

Moccasin

Old Fort Road

Sheep Head Ridge Road

Lighthouse Road

Big

Cape Romain NWR dock

Middens Trail

Beach Road

Turkey Walk

Lower Summerhouse

Summerhouse Road

Summerhouse Creek

Dominick House

Mill Road

Upper Summerhouse

Wildlife Viewing Platform

ATLANTIC OCEAN

February 20, 2003

0   1/2   1

Scale in Miles

I anticipate the marking of my birthday by a winter sail to Bull Island. Since I could not arrange work coverage for my birthday on Monday, I make plans to be off work on Thursday and Friday. Checking the tide tables, I see that Thursday will be the better day. My usual plan is to head over on the outgoing tide and return home with the incoming tide. With the low tide on the island at 4:20 p.m., I will wait a little for the flow to start before heading back to the mainland, allowing the water to be high enough on the Romain Retreat ramp to pull *Kingfisher* out.

This morning I make my preparations cleaning and inspecting *Kingfisher*. I collect the required equipment, preparing the sailing gear as well as clothing, footwear and supplies. For cold-weather trips over to Bull Island I take extra precautions, knowing I will be on my own for repairs, emergencies and other disasters. I also take a cell phone along, but mostly for my wife Susan's peace of mind. Several new pieces of gear are now essential in the kit: a waterproof bag that fits perfectly in the little stowage area aft, wetsuit socks and sailing gloves. Extra line serves an important function at my special "berth" on the island.

I pull *Kingfisher* the short distance from home to the landing. There is plenty of water on the ramp so I get off well and by two o'clock am outward bound on an outgoing tide. The wind is from the northeast, so going to windward on the way out Anderson Creek includes a few starboard hitches. I see one boat heading back home in the creek—this is to be the last person I see until Susan tonight. I am surprised when I enter Bulls Bay that the water is so smooth. The outgoing tide is giving me quite a push and the island approaches quickly. My plan is to bear off southwest down Bull Creek next to the island, continue into Summerhouse Creek and sail to the island's dock where I will secure *Kingfisher* and disembark for the island adventure. Earlier I wondered if I had overdressed with a foul-weather-gear top, but at this point the northeast breeze is picking up, the outgoing tide is creating some chop in Bull Creek and I am very happy to be dry.

Bull Creek is a major waterway that defines the backside of the northern end of Bull Island. The waters of the southern end of Bulls Bay flow into the extensive salt marsh creek system through Bull Inlet and the sister creeks Bull and Anderson. The section of Bull Creek I sail in now is also listed on some charts as Bull Harbor. From the Northeast Point to the penetration point of this creek into the marsh, depths between eighteen and thirty feet provided a fine anchorage for vessels in the past knowledgeable enough to navigate the shoals of Bull Inlet. A survey from 1696 by John Beresford labeled Bull Creek "Creek to the other Inlett," as an extension of Bull Creek unites Bull Inlet with Price Inlet at the southern end of Bull Island.

I make it to the Cape Romain National Wildlife Refuge dock on Bull Island before three o'clock, and execute a sloppy dropping of my sail in the water and a clumsy landing. I start muttering to myself about being a miserable plumber, and am reminded that this is a phrase I haven't used in years. A deceased friend Bob Held often used this phrase when not sailing too well. I remind myself of the respect I have developed over the years for plumbers and their required skills. I make all secure, and after changing clothes and pulling on my pack, set off for the interior.

When *Kingfisher* passed over the Intracoastal Waterway and entered Anderson Creek half an hour ago I crossed the boundary into the Cape Romain National Wildlife Refuge (Cape Romain NWR). As I step off the refuge's floating dock onto high ground, I am on the largest of the Cape Romain NWR barrier islands. The entire refuge spans twenty-two miles from Price Inlet on the south to the mouth of the Santee River on the north. The waters of Bulls Bay cover about half of the refuge's total area calculated at 64,229 acres. In Joseph Purcell's survey of Bull Island in 1793, the high ground was recorded as follows: "planting land," 1,357 acres; and "sand hills," 425 acres. The island's total area, including high ground, ponds, fresh and brackish water wetlands and salt marsh covers about 5,500 acres.

The maritime forest of Bull Island is one of the primary elements that elevate this natural area to its high reputation. A partial inventory of the botanical species of this subtropical forest—overstory trees: live oak, loblolly pine, magnolia, laurel oak, cabbage palmetto; understory trees and shrubs: sweet and red bay, wax myrtle, yaupon; vines: wild grape, yellow jessamine, Virginia creeper—does not flesh out the visual impact and sensory appeal of this veritable jungle. Bull Island has maintained this rich forest by the sea unlike developed islands like Isle of Palms. These sheltering woods provide for a range of diverse species. The allure of Bull Island would be severely diminished without the presence of its maritime forest.

It is the transition between the marsh at the western edge of the island and the maritime forest that I now walk through. There is a surprisingly large system of roads and trails on Bull Island, and I decide on a circuit route I have never traveled. Realizing my time is limited due to the late start, I plan to begin my return sail no later than 5:30 in order not to run out of light. After passing the open picnic area and Dominick House, I walk briefly on the Beach Road before turning left onto Sheep Head Ridge Road heading northeast. It is most conducive for hiking with cool and cloudy conditions. I am startled when I pass underneath a live oak and hear some creature in the tree above me. I react—something is airborne over my head and a huge owl appears on the wing heading away. I come to an intersection with a trail heading to the beach, my chosen route, and in the other direction I observe a large group of animals in the road. They come into focus—a flock of over a dozen wild turkeys.

Turkeys were introduced to Bull Island after they were trapped in the Francis Marion National Forest. Livestock was also brought to the island in the past and obviously could have free run on the high ground. Thomas Shubrick Sr. owned Bull Island during the American Revolution and had livestock on his barrier island plantation. A vignette from the Revolution references these animals. The Council of Safety knew of Shubrick's livestock on Bull Island, and, realizing the animals were easy supplies for British raiders, ordered Shubrick to drive the livestock off the island. After the unsuccessful naval attack by Sir Peter Parker's fleet in 1776, one of the departing ships confirmed the fears of the council when it raided the island. Henry Laurens, in a letter to his son John in England, communicated the following:

The Country Militia as well as the Town continued cheerfully to do duty on this frontier as long as one of the Enemy's ffleet remained in sight _ the Active was the last, she with a Tender went about ten days ago to Bull's Island the property of Capt Shubrick landed 40 White & 20 black Men killed by Platoon firing a few head of Cattle, augmented their black Guard by stealing Six more Negroes & then sailed off the Coast or perhaps only a little out of sight.

Whether the blacks were kidnapped or went willingly is a matter for consideration.

The habitat changes quickly as I head toward the beach, encountering wetland on either side of the trail. I soon scare up my next animal, a decent-size alligator that moves off the bank and back into the water. I was not sure I would see any alligators with the overcast skies. Another large alligator is ahead off the trail but out of the water, and despite my presence he doesn't move an inch. These swamp areas are filled with waterfowl, and they cackle and scoot off as I walk past. One of the beauties of a winter walk on Bull Island is the absence of biting insects and other pests—no-see-ums, mosquitoes, deer flies, greenhead flies, ticks and chiggers. In several months this same trail will be intolerable without protective clothing and repellant.

I cross Lighthouse Road and continue on a trail with pine-forested old dunes. Weathered and wind-sculpted shrubs lead me through the dunes to the beach. Cloudy and cool conditions rule. I find shells galore at the high-tide line, particularly whelks and cockles. I discriminately select a few as I head northeast with the plan to beachcomb and find another path back to the Lighthouse Road. The best shelling is up at the high-tide line, but I gaze down the beach toward lower water to look at something when I spot numerous sand dollars. I start noticing the time and begin looking for a path to the road. One likely candidate turns out to be a dead end, and I stop for a snack and sit by a fine young pine at the edge of the forest and dune system. Heading on, I allow five minutes to find the path or turn around to backtrack. My hopes are high when I see a road-size opening in the jungle of palmettos, pines and oaks; instead I find a creek stopping right at the beach and a disturbed small gator swimming away. This is not my path but luckily the real one is just beyond. I take one last glance out to the ocean and the bleached trees on the beach and notice again the absence of footprints anywhere on the island.

I must hustle, but there are interesting views all along some of the large ponds on the island. For such a small area Bull Island has a rich diversity of wildlife and habitats. There is no sign of red wolves today but they are present on the island. In 1977 Bull Island became part of the U.S. Fish and Wildlife Service's effort to restore the endangered red wolf population—an animal considered extinct in the wild—with a release of a breeding pair on the island. A breeding program for these wolves continues on the island, and the pups are raised in an enclosure. Mature red wolves are then relocated to Alligator River National Wildlife Refuge in North Carolina for their return to the wild. The Bull Island wolves have been noted to be good swimmers; one wolf island-hopped from Bull to Capers to Dewees and finally to Isle of Palms, where it was captured after finding prey around a golf course.

I encounter two white-tailed deer near the landing. There is such a sizable population of these animals on the island that a limited archery hunt is held annually each fall. Davis Thacher, a friend of one of the island's previous owners, Christopher Fitzsimmons, discussed visiting the island in his journal in 1817, and hunting the plentiful deer with hounds. At the dock I do not tarry as I work at getting *Kingfisher* rigged and gear stowed. I don't get underway until after 5:30, and soon after sheeting in, my traveler pops. One end is untied and I am not able to reeve the line through the fitting to retie. Instead I fasten the sheet onto the old unused wire traveler. Initially I have to sail to windward against the slowly flooding tide, but I decide to return on a different course, the serpentine ferry route. I round a point and bear off with the tide. It is still a nice breeze, and I expect an easy run on *Kingfisher* over to the Intracoastal Waterway in the remaining light of day, but this is not to be. I do well until several turns in the channel put me going to windward in a narrow creek against the tide. I try to hold each tack as long as possible but get more conservative after hitting bottom several times, hurriedly pulling up the daggerboard and tacking at the same time. I finally get through this gauntlet and follow a dolphin out to a wider area. It is definitely getting darker, and I have to take a careful look at stakes on the creek bank marking the channel. I go to port at one fork and realize quickly I need to go to starboard, bringing *Kingfisher* around into the wind and current again before I go too far. There are some beautiful moments when a red glow comes over the sky. I know this is the last gasp of light, but being bathed in this red light is sublime. It is the last light and I must refocus for night vision.

The illumination ahead is encouraging—the house lights of Romain Retreat and channel markers of the Intracoastal Waterway. I finally make it to the waterway, and start the beat up to the Romain Retreat landing. It is dark now and the breeze is light but steady. I don't have lights so I keep to the mainland side of the channel in case I need to duck away from any boats. But there are no other boats to be seen or heard, and I have the waterway all to myself. It has been some time since I have sailed in the dark, and I recall sailing at night at Wrightsville Beach, North Carolina, both in the Banks Channel and in the ocean by moonlight. The red light flashing every four seconds leads me finally to channel marker #68. This navigation aid is very close to the Romain Retreat pier, and I improve greatly on my sail drop and dead stick landing at the floating dock. So at seven o'clock I am back to civilization. As I haul out and head home, with the prospect of cleaning my act up and waiting for the next day to clean up *Kingfisher* and all the gear, I am already thinking ahead to my next journey to this beautiful, wild island.

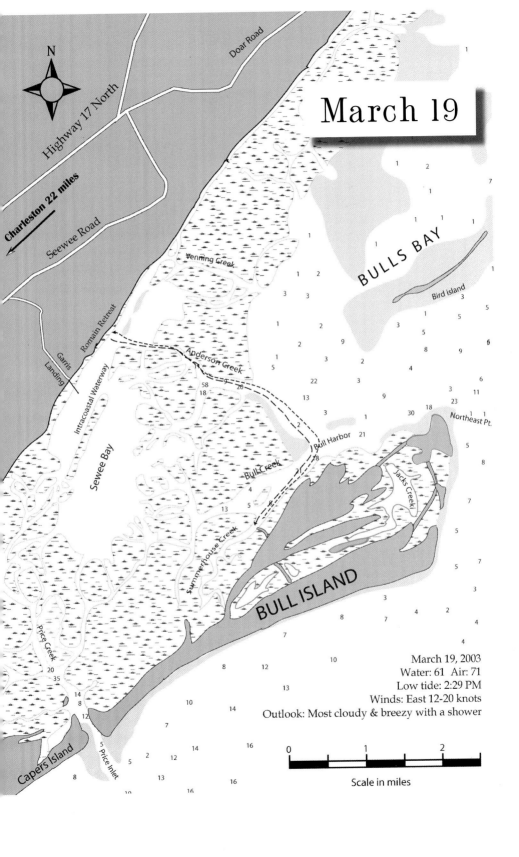

March 19

N

Doar Road

Highway 17 North

Charleston 22 miles

Seewee Road

Venning Creek

Romain Retreat

Garris Landing

Intracoastal Waterway

Anderson Creek

58
18   20

Sewee Bay

Bull Creek

Summerhouse Creek

Price Creek

Capers Island

Price Inlet

BULLS BAY

Bird Island

Bull Harbor

Northeast Pt.

Jacks Creek

BULL ISLAND

March 19, 2003
Water: 61   Air: 71
Low tide: 2:29 PM
Winds: East 12-20 knots
Outlook: Most cloudy & breezy with a shower

0   1   2

Scale in miles

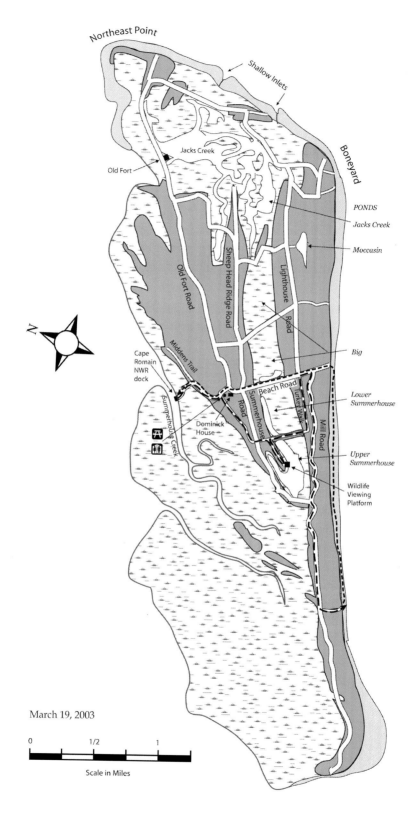

Northeast Point

Shallow Inlets

Boneyard

Jacks Creek

Old Fort

PONDS

Jacks Creek

Moccasin

Sheep Head Ridge Road

Old Fort Road

Lighthouse Road

Middens Trail

Cape
Romain
NWR
dock

Big

Beach Road

Summerhouse Road

Turkey Walk

*Lower
Summerhouse*

Mill Road

Summerhouse Creek

Dominick
House

*Upper
Summerhouse*

Wildlife
Viewing
Platform

ATLANTIC OCEAN

N

March 19, 2003

0   1/2   1

Scale in Miles

A day of dirty weather is in the forecast, but for some reason I have learned over the years to enjoy these conditions. After launching and securing *Kingfisher* at the dock, the boat's thin stainless steel rub rail catches on the underside of the dock frame and pops a rivet at the rail joint amidships. One side of the rail joint sticks out a foot. I am unable to locate a screw in my repair kit to refasten the rail. I reject upfront going home for repairs and commence a jury rig. It is not pretty, but functional in keeping the rail strapped to the hull. I rig up in a solid east breeze, and right before leaving the dock a head peeks around my raised sail. My neighbor Earl Grady voices concern (expressed by others) about my heading out into these waters in this little sailboat. I reassure him and am grateful for his push-off of my bow. As I head out Anderson Creek on a port tack, I am reminded of Earl's now deceased father, Ted Grady, and his past demonstration of how to get a boat in on a very low tide. He came across the waterway toward our landing years ago in his johnboat, maintaining a full head of steam until he reached the mudflats jutting out into the channel. At that point he tilted his outboard up until the prop was close to the surface, and ran that boat skimming across the pluff mud a good distance until it stopped at the solid bank. It was an impressive show by an experienced Lowcountry waterman.

Mist and a light shower are in the air as I come to the confluence of the main branch of the Anderson Creek and a side branch angling off to the southwest to the open shallow-water area now designated as Sewee Bay. This confluence has the local name of the Shark Hole, and a NOAA chart has the deepest depth listed as fifty-eight feet. Several miles to the south at a similar confluence in Dewees Creek is an even deeper Shark Hole (eighty-one feet). This hole in the marsh-estuarine system is the deepest location in Charleston County, deeper than any point in Charleston Harbor. My daughter Sara always viewed the Anderson Creek hole with some trepidation, "Are we past the Shark Hole yet?" The dark depths and the presence of sharks that breed deep below the surface always seemed to give the area a suspenseful aura.

Kingfisher quickly sails past the Shark Hole today and conditions continue to get wetter on entering the bay. No question about foul weather gear, and as the breeze picks up to twenty knots I begin to have difficulty discriminating where the spray stops and the rain starts. It is important to keep *Kingfisher* driving through the chop. It is not long before I am close enough to the island to consider bearing off to the southwest into Bull Creek toward the dock, but I make sure that in this breeze *Kingfisher* will not ground on a frequently-hit shoal. Seeing a stake to starboard I bear off and run into Bull Creek. Immediately *Kingfisher* is planing across the surface and down the waves created by the opposition of wind and tide. Several times I dip the bow underneath a wave and appreciate the Sunfish design; sailing in my old Laser here would have been much more dicey. The Laser tends to roll in these conditions, and the dreaded capsize to windward would be a horrible fate out here today. As I get closer to the dock the waters become calmer, but there is still a strong breeze. This time I have a fine landing, dropping sail and softly contacting the dock. Peering over my shoulder I note a boat coming out of the ferry route and swinging toward the dock. Two refuge staff members are aboard and bring the outboard into the restricted area of the pier. One of the staff comes over to figure out what I'm doing at the dock in the rain so early in the morning. The query begins with, "Are you OK?" and proceeds to whether I spent the night on the island. I reassure her that I am a local who sailed over in the morning. Turning the query around I inquire about their tasks for the day, and she replies that, weather permitting, they plan to spray phragmites. I offer my plan to walk on the southern end of the island, an area I have not traveled.

After carefully securing *Kingfisher* in her berth, I obsess over what gear to take, and with an ongoing drizzle bring my foul weather jacket for good measure. "South" is as detailed as my plan is, so consulting the posted map and distances I set out an approach: begin on the designated nature trail, swing over to the Beach Road, head south on the Mill Road, and find a way to make it over to the beach for a loop back. This walk through the forest will also be a good bug survey. The trail is actually a National Recreation Trail and has interpretive signage along its two-mile length. The nature trail faintly climbs and stays on a ridge, and soon brings a revelation about the island—there is topography and geology in these ridges and beyond. The ridges are former sand dunes, and the low areas in between have become sloughs and ponds. Studies conducted by boring sections of the island found that it is located on a topographic high underlain by rocks formed during the Tertiary Period. During a rapid rise in sea level, the relatively fast landward movement of an accreted sandbar was arrested when this young barrier island was grounded on the Tertiary high. Similarly, the presence of ancient (Pleistocene) river drainage systems provided the conduit for the modern tidal inlets, with Bull and Price Inlets defining the ends of Bull Island. Clearly this geological heritage provides the island with an underpinning lacking in the other islands of the Cape Romain NWR.

The trail meanders through a regenerating maritime forest of palmetto, oak and pines. There are occasional mosquitoes but overall it is a comfortable walk. The trail soon follows a manmade dike that separates a tidal creek from freshwater ponds. The first scuttle and splash I hear right before stepping onto the dike signals a reptilian presence.

On either side of the dike are the Summerhouse Ponds. Ahead is something dark on the dike, and I'm not sure if it is a log or a gator. It proves to be a five-foot alligator. This is not a wide dike, and despite my approaching presence he does not scuttle off. Taps on my water bottle are of no avail, and I wonder what is the protocol here? Finally, I pass by on the far side of the dike without eliciting any movement from the gator. Farther along on the dike there is a side trail leading to a wildlife-viewing platform. I decide to take the side trip and head down the trail that becomes a narrowing piece of land jutting into the Upper Summerhouse Pond. This finger of land is dominated by palmettos, and if not for the cleared path would have been a jungle. Many gnats are out but fortunately they are not the biting variety. I finally reach the platform out in the pond. This platform was obviously built for the viewing of migratory waterfowl, but today there are none evident.

Retracing my steps, I head back to the dike trail and continue on toward the east. Alligators are residing, and a large specimen slips into the pond on the right. There are numerous places where the movement of alligators from pond to pond have created paths like major thoroughfares, with hollows worn into the banks. The trail leaves the dike and heads back into the maritime forest on the beach side of the island. This path is designated as Turkey Walk Trail. Without sighting turkey here, I come out onto the familiar Beach Road and head right toward the beach. The plan is to go further south down Mill Road prior to exploring the beach. Right before the Mill Road a great noise—"thwack!"—explodes in a black water hole in the darkened woods. A dark head peers out of the water at me—this very large alligator has just expressed his displeasure at my presence by a great belly flop. I leave him and turn south down the Mill Road that leads all the way to the south end of the island. This road is planted on the shoulders with grain for wildlife. A turkey appears ahead and slips into the woods. Subsequently, a black racer slithers off in the same direction.

Rather than walk all the way to the south end before I loop back on the beach, I look for paths across to the shore. The beach is not far, since the sound of the surf is loud and prominent. I make several forays into the woods but am met with water barriers along the way. We have had considerable rain in the previous week creating high water levels, and I choose not to wade. I do my usual routine with setting a turnaround time, and soon find a wide road to the beach unmarked on any of my maps. Unfortunately sections of it are flooded. I notice the water is clear and not deep, and reassuring myself that a black object to the right is not a reptile I take off my shoes and socks and wade across. The clean cool water feels great on my bare feet. Once out of the water and heading onto a path through a wide set of dunes, I am greeted by sandspurs on my feet. I brush them off as the clouds overhead clear, and I am truly welcomed on the beach by the beaming sun and an above-average surf. I strip down to t-shirt and shorts, and settle down to lunch in this amazing setting. The foreground presents an awesome array of delights: shells of many varieties, a crab pot and various other items of flotsam and jetsam. The wonderful sun is framed by interesting cloud formations, and progressively the formations indicate more rain for the afternoon. But I am truly blessed to be in this moment.

Clouds covering the sun signal the time to shove on. I walk the high-tide line and occasionally dip down to the lower beach. It is truly a beachcomber's delight at both high- and low-tide lines. Everywhere is the gear of crabbers and shrimpers, and lumber—the fine raw materials to construct a nice shack and gazebo. A stout bamboo shaft becomes a perfect walking stick and perhaps a prod to poke away critters. The clouds continue to build and there are some signs of a decrease in the wind velocity. I search for the path to the Beach Road and finally come upon the prominent markings making it easy for beachgoers to find. The Beach Road is the return path toward the picnic area and the dock. Right after the intersection with the Mill Road, something black, green and huge appears in the road. This is the belly flopper, profiling his full hulk. Green algae from the pond dapples the deep black of his hide. What an animal! The tail is clearly half its body length and in all this reptilian descendant of dinosaurs appears twelve feet long. As I approach on the other side of the road, his tail swings to ninety degrees, and I interpret this action as his preparation to "turn tail" and hop back into his hole, but my stillness and lack of threat (despite my new bamboo stave) help him stay put. Finally leaving him alone with his tail back aligned with his body, I walk onto the dike separating Lower Summerhouse Pond and Big Pond.

A surreal image returns to my consciousness from my first trip over to Bull Island after Hurricane Hugo. The island, like my neighborhood forest, appeared to have been leveled by a nuclear explosion, and the maritime forest was shattered, defoliated, lifeless. Yet when I walked by Big Pond I became acquainted with the resilience of palmetto trees—the water was ringed with the lush greenery of the palmettos standing proud. They are still prominent today as are river willows growing along the dike and displaying the beautiful green of new foliage. Dominick House sits on this side of the clearing containing the picnic area, the weather shelter and restrooms, and the road to the dock. I experience a novelty for today, a group of people coming in my direction off of the afternoon ferry. My garb including long sleeves, hat, daypack and bamboo stick is in sharp contrast to a pair of women with shorts, blouses and cigarettes in hand. The other group of four includes a man with three teenage boys, and I inform them where to look for my belly-flopping reptile friend.

I head toward the dock, but remember my plan to take a look at the Middens Trail. Middens are accumulated piles of household refuse. The prehistoric middens of the southeast coast typically have shells (oyster, clam, whelk, periwinkle etc.) and often contain artifacts, including pottery fragments, lithic materials, shell tools and bone tools. In digging foundation holes for the pilings to support my house, I ran into layers of oyster shell and some potsherds. Martha Zierden of The Charleston Museum put the age of some of these pottery shards (Deptford Check Stamped) at a much older date than I imagined—around two thousand years old. I was stunned by this knowledge and prompted to further study the area's prehistory. The Middens Trail skirts along the western edge of the island close to the marsh and passes by several middens. This archaeological site (38CH40 – Indian Kitchen Midden Mounds) was nominated for the National Register of Historic Places, and when surveyed consisted of twenty small shell middens with an average size of one meter deep and three meters round. They are overgrown by the maritime forest, and in the survey some removal of shell for road fill was noted. These shell mounds are quite small relative to several over on the mainland.

The most prominent of the surviving shell mounds in Charleston County is the Sewee Shell Ring. It is one of a number of shell deposits with either a circular or semi-circular shape located along the South Carolina, Georgia and Florida coasts. These rings of antiquity have been dated to the Late Archaic Period, ranging from 4,600 to 3,000 years before the present. The Sewee Shell Ring is located less than six miles from where I stand. Just this year the age of this shell ring, through the use of radiocarbon dating, was given the age of 4,010 years (plus or minus 70 years) before the present, making it the second oldest shell ring in South Carolina. The function and meaning of shell rings has been the source of speculation and debate for some time. One theory hypothesizes the development of the ring by gradual accumulation of household refuse from a circular village with a central plaza. A second theory views the ring as a ceremonial construction, the ring builders living nearby but not on site. A hybrid theory posits both accumulation and ceremony as contributing to the ring's development.

An even larger mound once existed at the site of the Romain Retreat landing. This shell mound, known as the Andersonville Mound, was measured at fifty feet wide, three hundred feet long, and eight to thirteen feet deep. This important prehistoric site was unfortunately destroyed years ago before a thorough archaeological study when the shells were used for road fill. Native Americans utilized this location endowed with a natural sand spit that provided proximity to both the water on hard ground (not marsh) and a freshwater source running behind it. The other natural feature was the presence of the creek (Anderson) that leads to Jacks Creek and the Northeast Point. The existence of the Sewee Shell Ring, the Andersonville Mound site and the Bull Island shell middens indicate a regular presence of Native Americans for thousands of years on this island. Unfortunately the archaeological work on the island was done years ago, and is not up to current standards. The good news is that the lack of development on Bull Island has protected antiquities like these middens and presents the potential for future investigations.

On this trail today a troop of turkeys marches along, and whenever I come close enough to be visible they run ahead up the trail. Several times this occurs and becomes quite comical as the last turkey, with a bobbing head, motors just around the next bend. The path finally ends, and here I peer to the northeast and remember years ago bushwhacking from this area to the Northeast Point during the winter. I came across what sounded like a group of wild pigs but instead found a bird rookery high up in the pines. Returning from my reminiscence, I double back and stop at a view created by the downing of a large cedar of the marsh, water and mainland. This cedar has clear signs of Hurricane Hugo; having been twisted by incredible forces, it is in contrast to the resurgence of the maritime forest all around. I know people who have avoided coming back to the island due to the hurricane's devastation, and though plenty of Hugo's signs still exist, I mainly see rebirth and regeneration.

Prior to getting to the dock, I meet up with a man with a wetsuit and lifejacket walking up the road. I ask if he has kayaked over. He informs me that he has come over on a personal watercraft (PWC), the fastest way to get to the island; I do not dissent. The ferry *Island Cat* is also at the wharf with crew on board. I note the secure berth of *Kingfisher* and compare it to the awkward position of the PWC on the outboard side of the dock. It is time to rig and get underway, and my previous assumption about the diminishing wind is correct as the rain returns. I leave the bamboo hiking stick on the dock for a future hiker. Completing the final stowing of gear, with my sail up it is breakage time again as indicated by the curls of my sail on the boom. The end cap that secures the sail to the aft end of the boom has come off. So in the rain I drop sail and make repairs. After some finagling a satisfactory repair is completed, and I am finally underway.

Remembering my previous sail through the ferry passage last month, I choose to return by the same course as this morning. I hug the island side of Summerhouse Creek and then Bull Creek to stay out of the incoming tide, paralleling the Middens Trail and catching a view of the twisted cedar. There is an artifact on the bank of the creek, a piece of heavy equipment sitting sentinel, rusting and mired. Years ago a former refuge manager disregarded the warning of an employee and drove the bulldozer to its permanent home on this bank. As I approach the opening of Bull Creek to the bay, I notice on the island side a small point and the opening up of a cove to the right. I recall several pre-Hugo canoe trips into a small creek through the cordgrass, ending at the dike separating Jacks Creek impoundment from the marsh. A short portage allowed people to put their boats into this largest of the freshwater ponds on the island. With thoughts of entering the island again here, I bear off across the mouth of Bull Creek, and with a light breeze from behind and the push of the incoming tide head into the bay toward the home passage of Anderson Creek. This quiet glide homeward allows me to reflect on the conversation with the operator of the PWC. Hearing bird sounds and the exhalation of dolphins, I revel in my quiet passage, and in my choice.

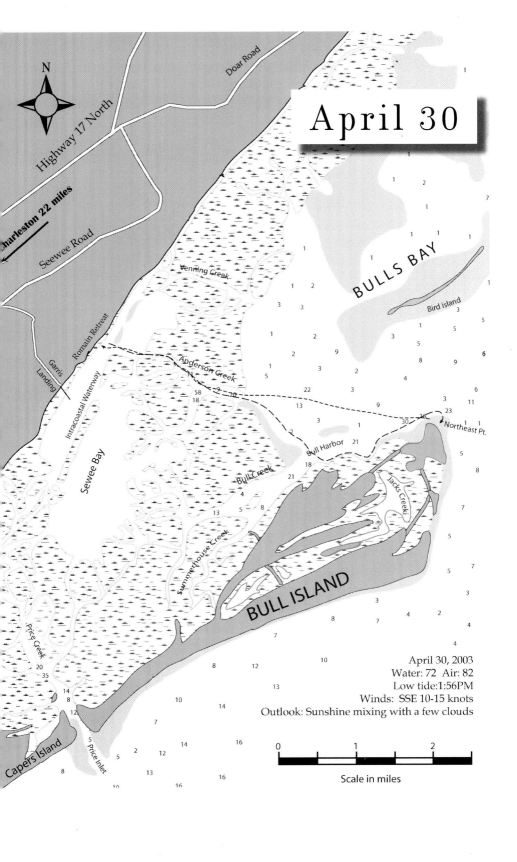

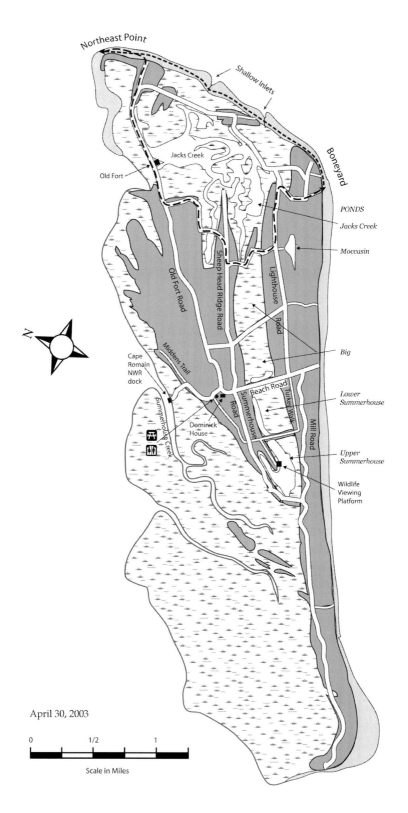

Northeast Point

Shallow Inlets

Boneyard

Jacks Creek

Old Fort

PONDS

Jacks Creek

Moccasin

Old Fort Road

Sheep Head Ridge Road

Lighthouse Road

Big

Cape Romain NWR dock

Middens Trail

Beach Road

Turkey Walk

Lower Summerhouse

Summerhouse Creek

Summerhouse Road

Mill Road

Dominick House

Upper Summerhouse

Wildlife Viewing Platform

ATLANTIC OCEAN

April 30, 2003

0   1/2   1

Scale in Miles

I get off to an inauspicious start this morning at 9:45 a.m. When I go to push *Kingfisher* off the trailer into the water, the bow handle I grab shears off at the deck. The aluminum has corroded through. My immediate thought is where to tie *Kingfisher*'s bowline, and I realize the base of the mast is as solid a place as any. A concurrent thought is the fact that I have been tying the boat off at this bow handle, and what a problem it would have been if the metal had sheared off and *Kingfisher* had come loose in a difficult situation. I also recall two years ago when sailing *Kingfisher* in a strong breeze on a reach to promote the maximum planing speed and hearing a gunshot-like explosion as the aluminum mast broke off about a foot above the deck. Luckily I was in the Intracoastal Waterway and had an easy paddle back to the landing. The failure of gear on boats is always a trigger for heightened anxiety and a reminder to take extra precautions.

The water is smooth and the wind variable. The bamboo stick I found in March gave me the idea of recycling my old Hobie 16 hiking stick, so I rig this new tiller/hiking stick and paddle out Anderson Creek. This extension allows me to steer from the forward part of the cockpit with my leg and have both hands free for paddling. The water has a scummy quality to it, and a loggerhead surfaces for a breath near the Shark Hole. I am sailing now as I reach Bulls Bay, and the open waters are still quite smooth. Today I will look to find a new access on the island via the creek into the marsh at the Jacks Creek dike. I was here years ago on several canoe trips, where we paddled to the island through a narrow creek in the marsh and portaged across the dike to the impoundment. I plan to find this creek, sail and paddle up to the dike, and leave *Kingfisher* at this new anchorage.

The wind is still light when I reach the marsh of the island, and I begin to search for the entrance. In the past this creek had handmade markers pointing the way and I look for these in vain. Several times I start up a creek, but it appears to be too small and I turn out. I am getting closer to the island and the dike of Jacks Creek is visible, but no entrance reveals itself. I am making my way north and finally realize I have gotten so close to the Northeast Point that there are no more creeks heading into the marsh. I decide to abandon the search and land at the Northeast Point. A different hike than my original plan begins to take shape. My current concern is finding something I can secure *Kingfisher* to at the point in order to hike on the island without fear of the boat washing off the beach. With a previous back injury to contend with, I do not wish to drag *Kingfisher* up the beach. Dragging my Hobie 16 catamaran up and down beaches for years probably contributed to my back problem. I searched for a partially buried tree on the point here last summer to tie off to but that search, too, was in vain. I have concerns about leaving *Kingfisher* here while making an extended walk into the island. Today at the point I find a snag above the high-tide line and am able to reach this with my long mooring line. So I set up this new berth, and notice that as far as I can see I have the island all to myself.

The Northeast Point of Bull Island is carved by Bull Inlet, a channel that provides some deeper water for access to the ocean, and in the opposite direction cuts across the large shallow Bulls Bay into Anderson Creek. Bulls Bay stretches about ten miles to the northeast where a series of islands make up the northern part of the Cape Romain National Wildlife Refuge. Here at the Northeast Point a panoramic view showcases marsh, mainland, bay, shoals of the inlet and the Atlantic Ocean beyond. The dynamics of the inlet and the great movement of sand have led to this new snag on the beach that meets my mooring needs.

It was on March 15, 1670, along this stretch of shoreline, that landfall was made in the historic encounter between the English settlers of the ship *Carolina*, and the Native Americans who inhabited this area, the

Sewees. The *Carolina* was the largest of a three-vessel fleet with the goal of establishing a permanent colony in Carolina. This ship was a seaworthy frigate, ship rigged, about one hundred feet in length and weighing two hundred tons. The *Carolina* was off course by sixty miles to the north of its intended landfall at Port Royal after an Atlantic voyage including stops in Barbados and Bermuda. Joseph West was in command of the colonizing expedition, and the governor to be of the new colony, William Sayle, joined the *Carolina* in Bermuda.

In the face-to-face contact on this point, the Sewees gestured the name of this bay "Sewee," and the name of this island "Onisecaw." The Sewees spoke some Spanish words to the English and welcomed them with their custom of stroking on the shoulders. One of the settlers was Nicholas Carteret, who recorded some of the details of the contact. In the second trip to shore, joined by Governor Sayle, the colonists were met by Sewees who walked out into the water to carry them to shore. The Sewee men wore deerskins and the women were "clad in theire Mosse roabs." They were taken to the habitation of the head of this group described by Carteret as "his Maty of ye place." The structure must have impressed Carteret and the colonists since he called it "ye Hutt Pallace." This "Maty" created some entertainment for the governor by carrying him on his shoulders to the lodging. Carteret was impressed with the "sauages" and their overall bearing. This second trip traveled to the mainland, as noted by Carteret "Some 3 leagues distant." One of the colonists on the *Carolina* was Stephen Bull, who later became a colonel in the militia of the province. Although he never held title to the island, he must have had some close association with it, for the island lost its Native American name and has been known as Bull or Bulls Island. Similarly, Sewee Bay became Bulls Bay, as did the other water places Bull Harbor and Bull Creek.

With *Kingfisher* snugly secured I pull out my gear for a hike around the Jacks Creek impoundment. My new tiller extension now plays the role of walking stick. I head up the beach around the point walking south. I soon run into a dead loggerhead on the beach, belly up and decomposing. I learn later that by midyear eighty loggerheads have been found dead on the beaches of South Carolina. While a few have obvious trauma marks from interactions with propellers and sharks, the cause of death of the others is not so clear. Biologists speculate two causes: hypothermia (caused by cold weather last winter) and pollution.

The northern end of Bull Island is composed of low-lying sand, marsh, the beginnings of sand dunes and dune vegetation until a bit to the south, where high dunes, higher elevation of sand ridges and the maritime forest start. The large dunes that starkly contrast with the low dunes I have just passed have been radically carved by storms and are topped by trees of the forest. This first high ground marks the entrance into the trail, road and dike system of the island that I plan to explore. I leave my sandals, and put on a pair of long pants and my all-terrain running shoes. I also apply bug repellant in anticipation of encountering a large crop of biting insects.

As if I sport a sign advertising fresh blood, I am greeted by a swarm of mosquitoes and deer flies about twenty steps into the forest. I pull my hat down around my ears and push on. My next greeter is quite a surprise—a five-foot alligator on the side of this forest road. It is an unlikely place for this reptile. I assume the countenance of a native Bull Islander and stroll casually past but am startled by quick movement and sound. When I turn I see open jaws and hear the hiss of his threat. I get the message and walk on down the road. I continue to notice the swarming biting insects as I move along. I expected mosquitoes today since I have quite a crop in my yard at home on the mainland, but the deer flies are also abundant. I decide I need the long sleeves of my windbreaker to protect my arms. This is the worst swarm that I can recall since a sailing and camping trip to Portsmouth Island on the Outer Banks of North Carolina back in 1977. A friend and I were the only humans on the island and were open season for the voracious insects. I also recall my first camping trips on the Outer Banks in the early 1970s, where we would prattle on around the campfire about the rationale for the existence of biting insects. Our buzzword for the collective of all biting insects was "scumbugs." We railed against their onslaught and the discomfort they inflicted on us. I have since learned that one reason for their existence is to control population. I have realized an additional benefit—keeping some natural areas wild by reducing visitors to the more prepared and hardy.

The road finally reaches the dike where it splits in two directions, and I take the fork to the right, the direction that becomes the Old Fort Road. The dike/road is grassy and has a natural hedge of predominately wax myrtle on both sides. On the road, a glimpse to the right peers out toward Bulls Bay, Bull Creek and the mainland. At a break in the myrtles on the left I look out to acres and acres of Jacks Creek, the largest impoundment on the island. A light south-southeast breeze is wafting through and provides a little relief from my insect pursuers. I push on down the road in the increasing warmth of the day and accompanying insects. I finally come upon an opening to the left that has a sizable vista to the pond. This opening contains the remains of walls built from tabby, a construction material made by burning oyster shells and used historically for foundations and buildings.

The site is known as the Old Fort, as is the road that leads all the way to Dominick House in the center of the island. The structure's origin and function are shrouded in mystery. While there is no historical documentation for the construction of this building, there are several documents that point to the "fort" being a watchtower. Speculation on function has also included fortification, a beacon and a gunpowder magazine. The General Assembly of South Carolina ratified an act on July 8, 1707, appointing eighteen "Look-outs" along the coast, and one was for Bull Island. Funds were appropriated for the salary of a "white man and two Sewee or other neighboring Indians" and the purchase of a canoe for these watchmen. Historian Alexander S. Salley hypothesized that the tabby foundation could be the remains of a watchtower. Others have further speculated that this could have been a Martello tower similar to those built along the coast of England and Ireland in the early nineteenth century as part of the defense against an invasion by Napoleon. But since these towers were only built at the beginning of the 1800s and the General Assembly act was passed in 1707, the jury is still out on the structure's provenance.

Adjacent to the tabby remains is a concrete and brick commemorative marker:

NEAR THIS SITE
THE FIRST PERMANENT EUROPEAN SETTLERS
OF SOUTH CAROLINA
LANDED ON MARCH 17, 1670
ON THEIR WAY TO ESTABLISH THE SETTLEMENT OF CHARLES TOWN
THEY ARRIVED ON THE SHIP
CAROLINA
FROM LONDON VIA KINSDALE IRELAND
AND BERMUDA
ERECTED BY THE SOCIETY OF FIRST FAMILIES
SOUTH CAROLINA 1670–1700
1978

I appreciate this commemoration of the 1670 landing. Some have taken exception to the placement of the sign since it appears to make a connection between the landing and the "fort." A real omission is the contact, the interaction between the English on the *Carolina* and the Native Americans, the Sewees. Throughout the island, the only acknowledgment of the significant Native American presence is the Middens Trail. What is important to note is that the "fort" and this monument both lie on what once was a marsh island, a bit of high ground that now is connected to the main part of the high ground of Bull Island by a dike.

There is a water-control device connecting the inlet at Jacks Creek to the salt marsh creek. Looking to the west here I note that one and a half hours before the low tide there is virtually no water in the creek, and several places in the shallow water have oyster clusters protruding. From this perspective, I realize that any future attempts to get in here would be sheer folly. In the past this creek was regularly used by fishermen who would come up the creek, leave their gasoline outboard engines on a rack, portage their boats across the dike and into the impoundment, and utilize electric trolling motors to fish for the freshwater species here. Hurricane Hugo breached the eastern dikes to the Jacks Creek impoundment. After the dikes were restored and the impoundment returned to its freshwater state the decision was made to keep it closed to access for fishing. The lack of traffic coming through the salt marsh entrance creek has probably contributed to the filling in of the small channel. The early maps of this area show this creek, called both Jacks Creek and Jackson Creek, being a prime access for this end of the island.

It was most likely into this creek entrance seeking shelter from a northwest gale that the young explorer and naturalist John Lawson entered by canoe with his party of other explorers and Indian guides, including Sewees, on January 7, 1701. Lawson had been appointed by the Lords Proprietors to make a reconnaissance survey of the Carolina interior. He and his party had spent the previous night on Bull Island and this gale necessitated a further night spent here. His later-published account of this journey, *A New Voyage to Carolina*, gives us an early and vivid picture of the island. Lawson also gave an account of native people, and his interactions with the Sewees led to his documentation of their history and sad demise.

I continue on the Old Fort Road until I find the crossroad heading to the southeast. Following this road and its winding path around the pond I come across a bird that is distinctive, unusual, but familiar. Looking it up later I find it is a black-necked stilt. It is one of a number of the many bird species seen on the island (close to three hundred) that I can recognize but not identify by name. I don't aspire to tick birds I observe off on a list, but I also recognize my desire to increase my knowledge and deeply explore the natural world. I continue my walk and in a smaller section of the larger pond I notice a plethora of popcorn trees surrounding this water. I push ahead to make my lunch stop at the beach, pass smaller freshwater ponds that are the upper reaches of Jacks Creek, and come to the path that leads to the beach. It is a path that has been built up by taking earth from the ditches on either side now filled with water. The path presents a wonderful tunnel of startling imagery, with the green maritime forest on either side connecting overhead, and the dazzling blues of sea and sky in the distance.

I come out of this forest tunnel and arrive at a most distinctive place on the shore. This location on the island is a point formed between the long ocean-front beach running to the west–southwest, and the shoreline running to the north. This point where the ocean meets the maritime forest is known as the Boneyard, named for the bleached hulks of trees littering the beach with huge "bones." Of the many photogenic settings on the island, the Boneyard is a top draw with the elements of ocean, sand, bleached tree forms, pools of water, light and shadow. I have worked up quite a sweat in the heat and long sleeves, so I strip down to my bathing suit and cool off in the delightfully refreshing ocean. The surf is small as I share the waves with vanquished trees. I have a relaxing lunch sitting on the beach, and before continuing my walk I cool off in the ocean one more time. I do not need to suit up again for a walk through the interior since the completion of the Jacks Creek circuit will now take me down the beach and around to the Northeast Point.

As I walk along I see my first people of the day. They are on a boat, fishing for redfish or spot-tailed bass at a popular spot around the base of submerged trees at the point of land. The action in the boat suggests they have a fish on. They appear to be about forty yards off the beach but close enough that they respond when I wave. I meander through the tree hulks on the beach, and, continuing past the Boneyard, arrive at the first of two shallow inlets, requiring me to remove my shoes and walk across barefoot. I come upon a section of a catfish body on the beach with an adjacent ghost crab hole. I cross the second shallow inlet and just beyond find the entrance to the trail system where I collect my sandals. I continue my walk around the point and note my anxiety to see the mast of *Kingfisher* in the distance. The source of my apprehension is a memory from years ago of a sailing trip to this same spot in my Hobie 16 catamaran. Two friends and I had left the boat on the point while we explored the beach. On our return we observed the Hobie sailing across the bay on its own, having floated off on the incoming tide. Our initial impulse was to try to swim to it, but this rash idea was quickly discarded. We finally found a boater willing to take us out to the Hobie. This experience is part of the reason I take such pains to find secure places to tie up, and I am glad now to see *Kingfisher*.

After rigging *Kingfisher* and stowing my gear, I shove off into the inlet and the incoming tide. There is a light wind as I run across the bay, and I occasionally paddle. The breeze is more solid as I reach the bay and I stow my paddle. As I glide through the curves of the creek I hear the exhalation of a loggerhead close to port. The brief glimpse seems representative of my limited knowledge and encounters with these distinctive reptiles. Where have the instinctive travels of this turtle taken it during its life? Is it feeding in the Anderson Creek marsh system? Is it looking for a mate? Is this a female that will be climbing the beach this summer to lay eggs? These questions pop up during a close second look as the turtle surfaces one more time and stares back at me. The reptile dives and is gone, and I silently slide back through the last section of the creek and across the waterway to my landing.

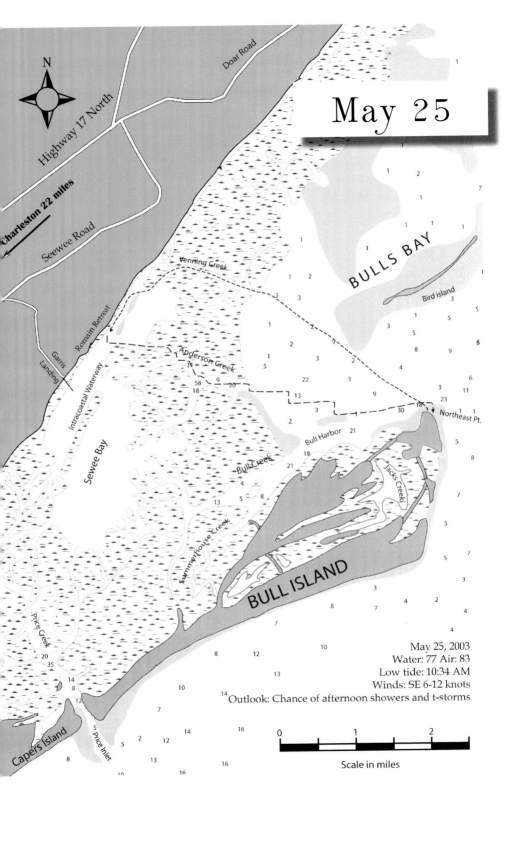

N

Highway 17 North

Doar Road

May 25

Charleston 22 miles

Seewee Road

Venning Creek

Romain Retreat

BULLS BAY

Bird Island

Garris Landing

Anderson Creek

Intracoastal Waterway

Sewee Bay

Bull Harbor

Bull Creek

Jacks Creek

Summerhouse Creek

Northeast Pt.

BULL ISLAND

Price Creek

Capers Island

Price Inlet

May 25, 2003
Water: 77 Air: 83
Low tide: 10:34 AM
Winds: SE 6-12 knots
Outlook: Chance of afternoon showers and t-storms

0   1   2

Scale in miles

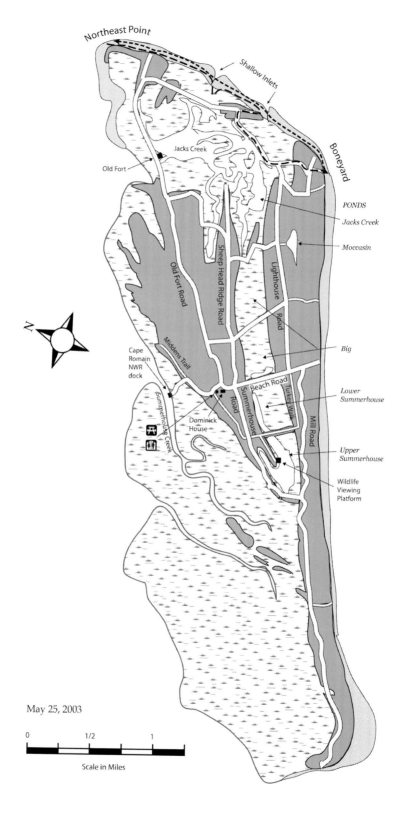

Northeast Point

Shallow Inlets

Boneyard

Jacks Creek

Old Fort

PONDS

Jacks Creek

Moccasin

Old Fort Road

Sheep Head Ridge Road

Lighthouse Road

Big

Middens Trail

Cape
Romain
NWR
dock

Beach Road

Summerhouse Creek

Summerhouse Road

Turkey Walk

Lower
Summerhouse

Dominick
House

Upper
Summerhouse

Mill Road

Wildlife
Viewing
Platform

N

ATLANTIC OCEAN

May 25, 2003

0   1/2   1

Scale in Miles

I have company at the landing when I arrive to drop off *Kingfisher*: Rich Shaw, the son-in-law of neighbors and his daughter Indy. They are talking about an alligator they have seen here this morning. When I return on my bike, prepared to sail, I see the gator floating off the dock. Additionally, before shoving off, I see an osprey, a dolphin and a small turtle, most likely a diamondback terrapin. This natural triad is a great sign for my trip. The wind is light from the southeast, but I have no need to paddle as I sail to windward through Anderson Creek.

With my early start I am receiving the push of the outgoing tide, and a lull in the wind before the Shark Hole is quickly swallowed in the now solid breeze. I come up closehauled, squeeze past an oyster point in the creek, and take in the outlook to Bulls Bay and the island in the distance. I make a last tack to fetch the mouth of the creek into the bay, slipping past the oyster point on the north side and a stake marking this shoal. *Kingfisher* is on the starboard tack and directly off the bow is the faint smudge of Bird Island shoal in the distance. Sailing as close to the wind as *Kingfisher* can point, I break out into the bay in pristine conditions marked by a superb clarity of the air. I'm lost in this reverie until wham!—*Kingfisher* comes to a dead stop with the sound of the daggerboard crunching into an oyster-laden shoal. I bring up the board quickly and work to get some way on before tacking toward deeper water when I am startled by a large dark body close overhead—a brown pelican gliding by. He could easily have been laughing about how I managed to run aground in this spot.

The course to the Northeast Point is directly into the southeast breeze. It is very fine sailing; the steady breeze is now about eight knots, the water is fairly smooth, and I am sitting on the side for trim. I continue the climb to windward and note that the push of the outgoing tide, especially in the deeper channel running out to Bull Inlet, is aiding my progress. But I stray by holding a tack longer to the southwest and scrape on the shoal on that side of the channel. I tack again and hold this closehauled course until my last tack to the island. I notice a motor sound close by and realize that this is the first observed boat today heading out into the inlet to fish. My landing on the point is also the first, a somewhat surprising fact since it is Memorial Day weekend. It is about forty-five minutes until the low tide, and all of the mooring line plus the main sheet is required to reach my newfound mooring, which is adjacent to a small outlet for the beach pool. After securing *Kingfisher* and packing up some items for my walk, I begin the hike up the island. Upon passing the beach pool, there is a splash and the flash of a marine tail. It is not a fish but a two-and-a-half-foot alligator. I wade in to get a closer look at this beautiful animal, and as it swims away in the clear water I observe the powerful tail as the mechanism for propulsion.

I walk around the point and past the remains of the dead loggerhead I saw here last month. There are also the tracks of one of the refuge's four-wheelers. Other boats head into the inlet to fish and one is coming back from the eastern point, probably from fishing the submerged snags off the Boneyard. I cross the first shallow inlet and walk in from the beach where this overwash of beach sand has fanned out. There are low sand dunes along here, and beyond is a section of salt marsh that stops at the dike marking this end of the Jacks Creek impoundment. The overwash has covered sections of marsh with sand, and as I walk farther back on this sandy finger I startle a wood stork. These large distinctive birds, with a wingspread up to five and a-half feet, have become fairly common in the Lowcountry and a regular sight roosting along the pond at Romain Retreat.

I have always been struck by this particular stretch of the beach of Bull Island, the area between the two shallow inlets. In the past this section of the shore has seemed confused and discombobulated but now a clearer picture has emerged. The dikes creating the Jacks Creek impoundment were built in the late 1930s. The purpose of building this 750-acre pond and a smaller one on Cape Island was to provide a conducive environment for wintering waterfowl in the Atlantic Flyway. A Civilian Conservation Corps camp was set up on Bull Island in 1937 for the purpose of constructing this impoundment. The CCC played a significant role during the Great Depression in providing the manpower and the finances to build major recreational areas in South Carolina. In this difficult time, young men were given the opportunity for work and education. The U.S. Biological Survey (now the U.S. Fish and Wildlife Service) planned these impoundment projects. Jacks Creek was a tidal creek running deeply into the back of the island from the western side, flooding and draining a large area of salt marsh. A natural marsh depression on this east end of Bull Island, already rimmed by higher ground for sections of the future pond, required the dikes to be built on the open ends to form the impoundment. The Army Corps of Engineers was also involved in this project and used a dredge and dragline to build up the 3,200-foot dike. CCC workers provided the considerable manual labor required. These dikes were erected to a height of 12 feet above low water, a distance planned to withstand a maximum hurricane tide. With the dikes and water-control devices in place and the salt finally flushed out, a number of aquatic plants were introduced into this freshwater environment, including widgeon grass, bull rushes, sago pond weed, wild rice, banana water-lilies, bushy pond weed, water shield and wild millet, to provide winter food for migratory waterfowl. At the time of this construction, the island had around 400 acres of freshwater ponds, both natural and manmade. The creation of a large portion of these duck ponds can be attributed to Gayer Dominick, the last private owner of Bull Island.

One significant impact of Hurricane Hugo on the island was the breaching of this dike in a number of places and the forming of an inlet right into the impoundment, changing it from fresh to saltwater again. More than a mile of dikes required repair, and the largest breach was three thousand feet wide. The actual breach was caused by the storm tide's rapid ebb. The dikes were eventually rebuilt and some areas hardened against future assaults from the ocean. This eastern side of Bull Island, running from the Northeast Point to the Boneyard, has been on the cutting edge of the erosional forces of the Atlantic Ocean. The current straight profile of this facet of the island stands in contrast to the curved arc of high ground shown on Joseph Purcell's survey for island owner Thomas Shubrick in 1793. The dynamic forces of nature and the constant wearing down from the movement of water in waves and currents have carved this island segment straight through. Coming south from the Northeast Point the first tall ridge of high ground is steeply scarped with a litter of trees at the base. At the far end, at the Boneyard, the bleached dead trees on the beach are the stark symbols of the violent interaction between ocean and maritime forest. In between the two points are two shallow inlets, paths for the ocean to have commerce with the marsh behind the very low dunes. Right in the middle of the two inlets are sections of peat protruding up from the beach. This exposed peat is an indication of the extensive beach erosion by waves that have exhumed salt marsh material once buried beneath the beach sands.

The signs of erosion are all around this side of Bull Island, but to the geologist the dynamics seen in movements of sand are part of the process of barrier island migration. The phenomenon of barrier island migration is in part a response to the rise of sea level, calculated to be at present a little more than 1 foot per century. Barrier islands move by erosion of the beach side, growth on the backside and maintenance of bulk and elevation. The range of the tide plays an important factor, and the barrier islands of South Carolina fall between the microtidal range (0–6 feet) seen in the Outer Banks of North Carolina, and the mesotidal range (6.5–13 feet) of the Georgia Embayment. Large ebb tidal deltas are associated with most inlets in South Carolina. The bending of the approaching wave fronts around the ebb sand shoals create the conditions necessary to form the classic "drumstick"-shaped model. Bull Island fits this model perfectly, with its wider northern section and narrower southern section. Cape Island to the north, in contrast, fits the "hotdog" mold, and due to its narrow, low profile and straight shore it experiences a considerably faster landward migration than Bull Island. Occasionally, the migration is accelerated by storms, as seen by the effects of Hurricane Hugo. The extent of shoreline erosion along the front beach of Bull Island was calculated to be 24 meters. Bull Island did not have any new channels cut through the entire island, excepting the breach in the Jacks Creek impoundment. A number of return surge channels were formed across the back and front beach but were noted to be filled with sand half a year after the storm. Orrin Pilkey, the noted coastal geologist, has concluded that hurricanes are important natural events that accelerate the process of sand movement, create new inlets and push barrier islands toward the mainland before they are flooded by the rising sea level. The movement of sand will continue, and the island will continue its slow march back toward the mainland.

I continue walking down the beach and move closer to the other shallow inlet. This is an excellent place to study the root structure of trees. There are a number of pines on the beach, and several have five feet of exposed root system. Seeing this exposed root structure helps one understand why Hugo's winds snapped off most pines rather than uprooted them, which was the fate of many oaks and hickories on the mainland, including a majority of the mature trees on my property. This area of remnant pine stumps on the beach is part of a hammock of slightly higher ground between the two shallow inlets. Before I reach the other shallow inlet there is another section of large overwash pushing sand far back into the marsh and close to the dike. I stop before the inlet to take a snack break and contemplate my plan. My options: hike up the beach to the Boneyard and beyond searching for early turtle crawls, and then on my sail home make a side trip to Bird Island shoal; or take a longer hike into the road and dike system. I decide to do perhaps a little bit of both, walking in to the dike here, walking across to a path through to the Boneyard and coming back down the beach.

Preparing for biting insects, I suit up with a pair of lightweight long pants. I enter the dike system through a trail angling back to the north on the end of the pine hammock before the second shallow inlet. There are a few biting flies waiting for me in the short walk through the hammock, and when I reach the dike I turn left to the south. This elevated area has an open view of the ocean, over the marsh and dunes between the dike and the beach, and a view in the opposite direction of the large impoundment. A pair of birds, a great blue heron and a great egret, fly off from the freshwater, and several alligators swim nearby. The southeast breeze is blowing across the elevated dike, keeping the biting insects off, so the walk is very pleasant. I walk onto the end of the dike and continue on down the road until the intersection with the Lighthouse Road.

About ten years ago I received a gift of a historic photograph. It is a black-and-white image, dated 1885, and labeled "Bull Bay Lighthouse." In the center of the picture is a house of similar design to mine, a saltbox. There are chimneys at either gable end, and at the center of the roof peak a modified cupola topped by a round deck with the beacon above. The yard appears mainly sand, and to the left there is the rise of sand dunes with vegetation and palmettos beyond. A tall picket fence surrounds the house and is fronted by a shorter picket delineating a yard. In the center of this yard stand four figures: two small children and possibly a mother and infant. In the right background is another small building, and seen just above the tall pickets is the dark figure of a man. The photo appears to capture the lightkeeper and his family. The ten-acre plot of land for the lighthouse was sold to the United States government by Charles Jugnot in 1851 for $200. The deed also specified that the government would have the right to land on nearby Jackson Creek and access for carts and wagons to be drawn along the shore. A new site slightly north of the abandoned one was approved by the Lighthouse Board in 1897, but the plan for a new lighthouse here was shelved. A U.S. Geological Survey map from 1919 confirmed that the site of the abandoned lighthouse was near the Northeast Point around the east side. Similar to the Morris Island Lighthouse, the actual physical location of its foundation is now off the beach under the water, but the Bull Island lighthouse has long ago disappeared.

Currently I follow one of the several outlets to the Boneyard. This path takes me straight out to the point where a fisherman is anchored off the snags. This is clearly a hot fishing spot, as I often see boats at this isolated area. I shed my long-sleeve clothing and walk back to the north on the beach picking through the tree-littered Boneyard. Clouds are building over the mainland, and a thunderhead is making up over McClellanville. I will keep watch on this development; I recall last summer being caught over here during a thunderstorm when I secured *Kingfisher* and took shelter in the low dunes of the Northeast Point until the mild thunderstorm passed.

Before I arrive back at the most southerly shallow inlet I notice a familiar sight: a large group of birds, including pelicans, black skimmers, terns and other shorebirds, standing at the water's edge. They appear waiting . . . for what? I learn later that this is termed a low-tide roost. I decide this distinctive place needs a name, so I coin the phrase the Waiting Beach. I wade across the shallow inlet and my familiarity with the island in large and small ways comes to mind when I notice the bleached cedar tree on the beach where I earlier sat for my lunch. Farther on down the shoreline I also recognize a lone oak tree still standing proud on the beach. This is the tree I picked out in the past as a place to land when I sail around the Northeast Point and down the beach. It is not just a stout place to tie onto, but also marks a place where I can land through the surf without encountering any submerged trees. I graced this tree in the past with a name too—Landing Oak.

I carry on and cross the other shallow inlet. I keep up my pace to check out *Kingfisher* and watch the developments of the thunderstorm across the bay. There are other people on the beach walking on the shoal of the point. I exchange greetings with a couple that is heading up the beach to shell. There are more boats around the point with picnicking families on the beach. It is time to finish my lunch and go for a swim in the inlet's sharp drop-off. *Kingfisher* is ten feet from the water but the incoming tide is advancing up the beach. A thunderstorm is still a possibility, and some of the picnickers are packing up and heading back to the mainland. This is the most people I've seen on the island all year, but I remind myself that it is Sunday of Memorial Day weekend.

With the lingering threat of the storm to the north and considering the time of day, I abandon my plans of sailing to Bird Island. Even with the clear weather, I can't see it from the Northeast Point. I don't have a chart with me, an omission I plan to rectify on future sails. Thinking ahead for further exploration, I plan my return sail not via Anderson Creek but instead Venning, another deepwater creek through the marsh a bit to the north. I shove *Kingfisher* off from the shore and set a heading across the bay toward my recollection of the mouth of Venning Creek. At a minimum I hope to get a better idea of the location of Bird Island. *Kingfisher* is running with the southeast breeze across the smooth bay, and it is effortless sailing. My course in this direction across the bay is keeping me away from the Memorial Day boat traffic running to and from the Northeast Point. Halfway across the bay, Bird Island is visible to the northeast. I am already downwind so I make a mental note of the bearings for a future trip. There is an appeal to venturing to this desolate sand spit away from boat traffic. A johnboat off my stern, heading in that direction, is a disturbance to my fantasy, but his progress is hampered as he begins to churn up mud in the shoals and he turns around.

As I reach the juncture between the bay and the beginning of the marsh, I am not far off of my reckoning when I spot stakes marking the creek entrance a bit to the west. I jibe and reach over to the creek mouth, glide into the entrance of the marsh, and feel the wonderful embrace of this tidal creek's inviting nature. *Kingfisher* is still running before the wind and the tide is pushing more in the restricted waterway of the creek. I meet a fine-looking outboard coming out, and he slows down to marvel at how I have the elements with me for a swift run.

"Yes, wind and tide," I reply, and he continues heading out toward the bay.

Kingfisher is finally through the creek and into the tiny sound behind the banks at the edge of the Intracoastal Waterway. She sails out through the familiar channel between shoals into the waterway on a last reach for the dock. The thunderheads in the distance toward the west are still present but no longer a worry. The end of my sail today is imbued with immense satisfaction and pleasure.

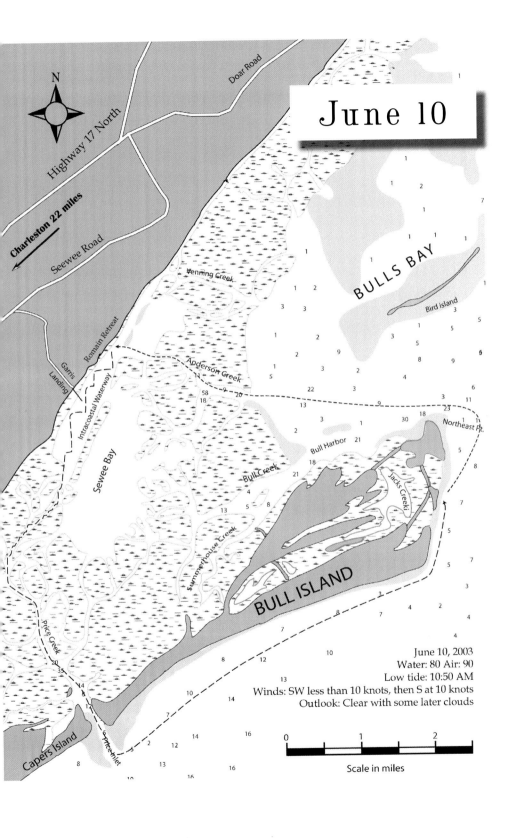

June 10

Charleston 22 miles

Highway 17 North

Doar Road

Seewee Road

N

Venning Creek

Romain Retreat

Garris Landing

Intracoastal Waterway

Anderson Creek

Sewee Bay

BULLS BAY

Bird Island

Northeast Pt.

Bull Harbor

Bull Creek

Jacks Creek

Summerhouse Creek

BULL ISLAND

Price Creek

Capers Island

Price Inlet

June 10, 2003
Water: 80 Air: 90
Low tide: 10:50 AM
Winds: SW less than 10 knots, then S at 10 knots
Outlook: Clear with some later clouds

0   1   2

Scale in miles

I drop *Kingfisher* in the water at 6:45 a.m. and note the glassiness of the Intracoastal Waterway. I watch as a fisherman roars by and swings into Anderson Creek heading out. Back home I watch the wind on the trees, especially a nicely progressing hickory tree, and look for signs of a breeze. I recall a childhood memory of the movement of leaves and branches in the trees in my backyard as the wind speed picked up, and an associated anxiety related to sailing in strong winds. Satisfied that the breeze is slowly coming today and aware of the tide milestones, I come back to the landing at 8:30 on my bike and am underway with a light southwest wind at 8:45. I begin tacking down the waterway to the south to undertake a long-awaited voyage—a circumnavigation of Bull Island. My sail plan, which I wrote down and shared with my family, consists of heading south to Price Inlet, taking the outgoing tide to the ocean, heading northeast paralleling the island's coast, continuing the sail around to Bull Inlet and the Northeast Point, and back across Bulls Bay and into Anderson Creek to the landing. It is an ambitious plan, but carefully coordinated with the tide changes and an excellent weather report for the day. Still, some anxiety is present as I recall previous sailing adventures and mishaps.

One very naïve sailing voyage during my college years took place at Ocracoke Island on the Outer Banks of North Carolina. Camping there with several friends, my plan was to sail from Silver Lake around the southern point with a friend, Jim Smolen, as crew (ballast). Proceeding down the ocean side, we would land at the northern end near the ferry landing. It was an ill-conceived plan, but I was an adventurous sailor who had developed a level of skill to not only relieve my former childhood anxiety about windy conditions but also to revel in them. The next day brought gale-force winds, and the ocean was a wild scene. I chose a relatively more prudent course of sailing on the sound side down the length of the island. With reefed sail and crew aboard, we tore off running with the wind. The Laser began to roll side-to-side then quickly and violently capsized to windward. Jim, coming up out of the sound, had a panicked look on his face. We righted the craft and bore off again with the same upside-down result. We realized we were in very shallow water, and a chart would have shown more shoaling (perhaps impassable) on my chosen course. Leaving valor aside we righted again, headed back for the landing, and made it without further mishap. Our other friend was waiting for us, and he stated that he had been debating when he would visit the local coast guard station to inform them that his two friends were in the process of trying to sail a fourteen-foot sailboat down the island in the "Graveyard of the Atlantic." This misadventure still brings forth laughs.

A little after nine, as I pass Garris Landing (the former Moore's Landing), I see *Island Cat* backing out of its berth and into the waterway with a group headed to the island. We wave as we head in opposite directions. Soon I meet other craft also heading opposite me. Some of these vessels are "snowbirds" steaming quickly to the north. I give way into the shallows, and my effort is rewarded with skippers slowing down to prevent the swamping of my poor little sailboat in their wake. I have picked up crew, the usual greenhead flies, and am occasionally annoyed by their bites. Beating through some holes in the wind but still having the push of the outgoing tide, I finally make the entrance to Price Creek. Though I have only a few experiences sailing by here, there is clear sign that this is the gateway to the inlet, and a loggerhead breathing nearby bodes well. I now no longer need to tack but reach closely through this fine wide creek, deep in the low tide of the salt marsh. The water is smooth and I mostly have it to myself in these reaches except for the herons and egrets on the oyster-shell bank. I pass by the incongruous buildings of Little Bull's Island and see fishing boats ahead flanked by the sandy banks of the islands Bull and Capers. I speak to the men on the first boat as I glide by and learn they have caught several flounder. The next fishermen are anchored farther out in the inlet but still inshore, and they have been catching small sharks. I express to them my hope that I don't find any big ones outside and continue heading out with the last of the falling tide.

With fishing boats behind I continue my push out the inlet. Venturing into inlets is always exciting at the juncture of the funneled waters flowing between two barrier islands and the ocean. This is an absolutely gorgeous day with light to moderate breeze and small swells outside. This is the perfect day to make this outing for the first time, and to study the geomorphology of the inlet. Price Inlet has historically demonstrated the dynamic nature of inlets with its channel shifting, widening and decreasing in depth over time. The shorelines of the ends of Capers and Bull Islands have changed in a cycle as the main ebb channel has shifted in its passage through the ebb-tidal delta, the large underwater sandbar sitting off the mouth of the inlet. Like the adjacent barrier islands, Price Inlet is also in an ongoing process of migration. Its main visual impact today is beauty, with the deep blues of the channel contrasting with the light blues of the shallows. Inlets can be treacherous places for the unwary, and have been the repeated scenes of drownings. Inlets in such tourist destinations as Sullivan's Island (Breach Inlet), and Wrightsville Beach, North Carolina (Masonboro Inlet), are marked by large signs warning people not to venture into these waters, even for wading.

A high drama played out in Price Inlet on a July day in 1955. The Magwood family lived on Little Bull's Island at this inlet, and on this day the head of the household, Clarence, had gone to the mainland for supplies. Left on the island were his wife, Ethel, and two of their children, Earl, thirteen, and Mary, eight. Earl had gone to check on a bateau he had used as a float for a shark set line. He found the boat submerged and was not able to haul up the anchor alone. He sought help from his mother, and they returned in another bateau with an outboard engine. They both went to the bow to try and haul up the anchor, but water came over the bow quickly. Before they knew it the boat had swamped, sunk to the bottom with the weight of the outboard and left them on the surface on a fast-ebbing tide similar to my outgoing tide today. Fortunately, an oar surfaced for them to grab, as Ethel was a non-swimmer. Earl held on to his mother and the oar as the tide took them out toward the ocean. She told him several times to just save himself and let her go but he refused. After some time they found themselves on one of the sandbars in the inlet, most likely the southwest channel bar. Though able to stand they were still separated from Capers Island by a deep channel. After resting, Earl was able to propel his mother holding on to the oar across this channel to the beach of Capers, and from here they walked around to Price Inlet. But a water obstacle still separated them from their home, the deep tidal waterway Schooner Creek. Ethel told Earl she could not go back in the water again so he swam the creek, slogged across the marsh and made it to their island home. He grabbed another bateau with a motor and returned to the inlet to pick up his mother. Ethel had been very concerned that her daughter Mary was left alone at home. The young girl knew something was terribly wrong when her mother and Earl were gone for so long, so she maintained a vigil in front of a painting of the Last Supper, praying for her mother and brother. When Ethel ran into her home on her return, she found Mary asleep.

Today, though the surf is small there are still breakers on both sides of the shoals, and this wild inlet could easily kick up to produce the conditions referred to by mosquito fishermen of the Charleston Inlet as the sound when the "Charleston bar be moaning." I have no reconsideration of my plans with these relatively gentle conditions. The shoal on the updrift (Bull) side is very long, perhaps reaching out a mile from the island. There is almost water enough to consider cutting across here before going all the way outside, but I note the small break of swells on the far side of the shoal and decide to continue with the few tacks needed now to go all the way to blue water. Finally passing outside of the shoal, several swells I sail over break off to port in the shallower water, but I come outside dry and clear. A surprise out in the blue ocean is the traffic: there is a quartet of shrimpboats outside of the head of the inlet. I am able to pick out a dozen boats from along Bull up the coast toward Isle of Palms and I learn later that this is the first day of the shrimp season for commercial shrimpers. I read later that the catch of the more-favored roe shrimp (white) is slim, but the catch of the smaller brown shrimp is much better, with one boat reporting a haul of two thousand pounds today. Hearing of this catch reminds me that in these waters are many living creatures, but the ones most visible as I begin my run down the coast are cannonball jellyfish and bottlenose dolphins.

Since several of the shrimpers are taking a drag closer to the island, I select a course toward the Boneyard point where the island makes a turn to the north and goes straight up to the Northeast Point. I find a new companion for this leg of the voyage, a bumblebee that keeps buzzing near my head. After moving past the shrimpers, I angle farther in toward the beach to search out a glimpse of the path to the Beach Road. Though still off the beach a half-mile I use the island tower in the distance to sight for the path, and the presence of a couple and their child frolicking in the surf is a good indication of the path's location. As I am blessed with cloud cover on this hot day, I continue angling closer to the surf and begin to see bait fish snapping on the ocean's surface just outside the surf line. Brown pelicans and cormorants are diving and fishing successfully here. At the point of the Boneyard I am able to see several of the paths leading into the island's interior, and I make the turn at 12:15, completing my run down the island in a little over an hour in this mild breeze. I continue to run just outside the surf and sail by the Waiting Beach. I look ahead for a favored landing site on this beach and identify the Landing Oak standing up straight out of the sand. I run in through small surf, and two breaks put me right up on the sand ten feet from the oak. I drag *Kingfisher* up a bit, leave my sail up and cool off in the surf before settling down for lunch on the beach. As I walk around the high-tide line after lunch, ever the beachcomber, I note the circling and crying of one, then two birds around me and back over the washover area before the marsh and dike around Jacks Creek. After doing a double take I recognize these as black-necked stilts and remember seeing a pair in Jacks Creek in April.

The incoming tide reaches *Kingfisher*, beckoning me to set sail and complete the island rounding. I could easily have slid down the beach and through a little channel to enter the inlet and round the Northeast Point, but I look out to the breakers at the end of the inlet and decide to round out where the *Carolina* probably entered in 1670. This outward course brings up memories of another past sailing adventure, but unlike the Ocracoke debacle there is no humor laced in the memories. On a December day in 1974 at Wrightsville Beach, North Carolina, I set sail in my Laser on my usual course south in the Banks Channel headed toward Masonboro Inlet. This inlet contained a jetty on the north side (there are now jetties on both sides) and shoals with surf on the south toward Masonboro Island. This was not a typical day since an offshore storm had kicked up a huge swell, and an experienced surfer estimated the surf at eight to ten feet. My intention was to make a circumnavigation of Wrightsville Beach, and a fresh southern breeze was right for the plan. I was prepared to take on the most challenging conditions of high winds and large waves. I wore a full wetsuit and had developed my inlet- and ocean-sailing skills through many hours and days on the water. Still, as I headed out the inlet on the outgoing tide I was startled by the size of the waves rolling in all around—a huge break farther out than I had ever seen on the southern shoals and swells easily peeling high over the jetty to my left. But with conviction and skill, I surmounted each of the swells in the Laser. I cleared the jetty and bore off to the north to make my way down the beach to the other end of Wrightsville and Masons Inlet.

In the cold December North Carolina waters I kept well off the beach, since the huge swells were breaking farther out than I had ever seen. Even so some of the swells out half a mile and beyond were still becoming critical and breaking. As I flew down the coast, often taking waves and wildly surfing along, I looked for these breakers. Sure enough a wave broke on me, capsizing me to windward in the open sea. Using my ocean experience I held on to the end of the sheet and like a surfer using a bungee cord pulled myself to the craft, righted it, jumped in and flew off. My commitment didn't waver and I was having the ride of my life, bringing adjectives of other adventurers to mind: surfers' "gnarly," and rock climbers' "sick." I flew past both of the fishing piers to I'm sure gaping onlookers and down to the northern end of Wrightsville and the untamed Masons Inlet. I knew I would find my greatest challenge there since I had seen the inlet in typical conditions with surf breaking all the way across the inlet. But I was not prepared as I drew closer to the inlet for the sight ahead: a large area of huge waves breaking far off the beach and inlet. I was prepared to utilize my breaking inlet and surfing experience finding my way through here to the safety inside the surf line. I had to avoid the massive breakers and try to find a line to surf through on a large but manageable wave. I kept avoiding taking the largest waves by heading up and out to the open sea, but as I got closer to the inlet this became more difficult.

With finality the biggest wave I had ever seen loomed outside of me and was so critical I had no chance to make it over the top. Without alternative I bore off to take the wave, and surfing quickly turned to flying on the rapidly building wave. I was going so fast I surfed right through my sail, and the sail and boom were vibrating directly amidships as I careened on this wildest of rides. I had to hold onto each side of the cockpit to keep the craft trimmed correctly. Then the wave released all its energy and fury in a great crash, and I experienced the worst of sailing violence—the pitchpole. The bow was sent straight toward the bottom and the speed of the craft and the wave tripped the hull end upside down. I was catapulted forward, and having no hold on the sheet I reached out for dear life for any piece of the craft, but my handful of sail was ripped from me. I was underwater in a storm-surf-filled inlet far off the beach, and all my experience and training went out the window. I panicked, sensing that I could be in a life-or-death situation, and my instinct was to get to my boat. There was a good deal of separation between the boat and me. Though the wetsuit contributed to my fatigue it was a lifesaver that day. I finally made it to the craft, and several attempts at righting the boat were unsuccessful due to the pounding waves. Finally I got the Laser upright and seeing that the mast was not broken I was ready to get her underway and out of danger. But something was terribly wrong with the boat—the mast was not secure in the fiberglass step in the hull, and as the mast continued to make uncharacteristic movements it started to actually crack the deck open. I found a way to pull the mast down and worked at securing the disarray. I tried to keep the stern square to the waves, which were not the beasts of the outer break but the surge closer to shore. Having no sense of the time I spent in crisis, I came to shallow water and pulled my wounded craft up on the beach. Exhausted from the physical and emotional demands, I sat quietly on the boat with mixed emotions. Having seen some of the drama, a lone beachcomber came over to see if I was all right, and I could barely respond. Though almost thirty years ago, the memories of that scene remain vivid to this day. As a postscript to this story, on June 14 the *Taki-Tooo*, a thirty-two-foot charter fishing boat, was heading out the inlet at Tillamook Bay in Oregon for a bottom-fishing trip. In ten- to fifteen-foot waves the craft was hit broadside by a huge wave and capsized. Nine aboard, including the captain, were drowned and another two remained missing.

So I now approach this wild inlet on a gentle day, though the sea breeze is beginning to freshen. I note a couple of surfcasters near the Northeast Point as I head out to the terminus of the southern shoals in cloudy conditions. When I get out to the end of the shoals I notice their broadness, and I am not even able to see where I need to turn. A sailorly instinct tells me to jibe and head back toward the point, and after the turn I realize I am almost closehauled. Running farther around the shoals would have me beating back into the inlet. No, it is time to head in and I pick my way through these shoals by avoiding areas of breaking waves. I make it to the smooth protected waters without getting wet, and to answer this dryness a shower begins to sprinkle me with cool fresh rainwater. I pass the Northeast Point at 1:30 and cruise into the smooth bay with closely trimmed sail. I pass the surfcasters' boat, the only other craft in the area, and am escorted for some time by a pod of dolphins. Several times I muse at extending the sail to other courses but continue toward my home passage into the Anderson Creek. I am greeted at the creek mouth by a great jump of a sparkling bluefish then farther on by a second loggerhead sighting. The brief shower is over, and the end of this voyage is brought home in the serenity of the marsh and creek, with the fine sea breeze and incoming tide pushing me easily to the landing. After securing *Kingfisher* I cruise home on my bike, content with the day.

I return to the landing later with my son Eliot to pick up a cell phone from my water bag and realize the sea breeze has continued to build. I am still awaiting our van with trailer hitch to pull *Kingfisher* home and spontaneously decide to rig for a short sail in the freshened breeze. I beat south in the waterway as in the morning, but with the higher tide and wind, *Kingfisher* picks up speed as I assume a performance mode of sailing. The physicality of sailing the boat is a pleasure, and for years has been my gym for strength training. I sail the boat hard, hiking to keep the craft trimmed and tacking the boat smartly with a timed movement under the boom to the new windward side. So the brief encore sail punctuates another memorable day on the water around the island.

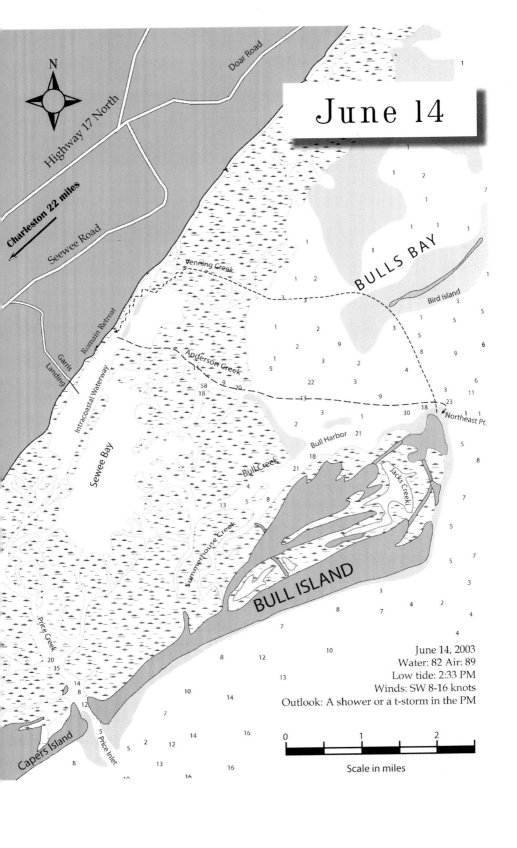

June 14

N

Doar Road

Highway 17 North

Charleston 22 miles

Seewee Road

Venning Creek

Romain Retreat

Garris
Landing

Anderson Creek

Intracoastal Waterway

Sewee Bay

Bull Harbor

Bull Creek

Summerhouse Creek

BULLS BAY

Bird Island

Northeast Pt.

Jacks Creek

BULL ISLAND

Price Creek

Capers Island

Price Inlet

June 14, 2003
Water: 82 Air: 89
Low tide: 2:33 PM
Winds: SW 8-16 knots
Outlook: A shower or a t-storm in the PM

0   1   2

Scale in miles

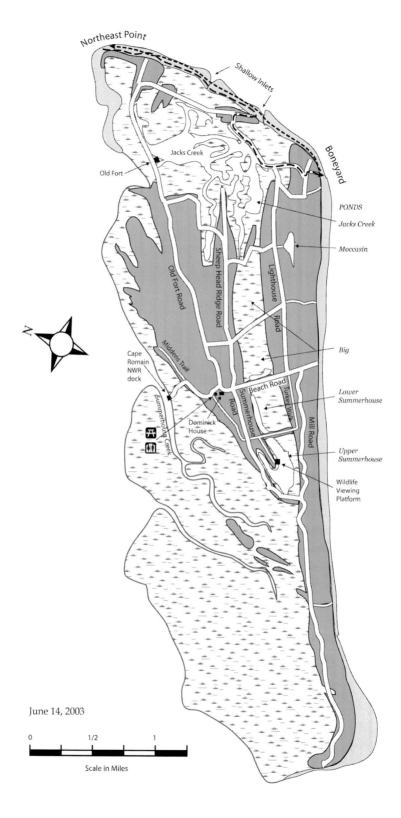

Northeast Point

Shallow Inlets

Boneyard

Jacks Creek

Old Fort

PONDS

Jacks Creek

Moccasin

Old Fort Road

Sheep Head Ridge Road

Lighthouse Road

Big

Middens Trail

Cape Romain NWR dock

Beach Road

Lower Summerhouse

Summerhouse Creek

Summerhouse Road

Turkey Walk

Mill Road

Dominick House

Upper Summerhouse

Wildlife Viewing Platform

ATLANTIC OCEAN

June 14, 2003

0   1/2   1

Scale in Miles

The fine high pressure that created the excellent conditions for my circumnavigation of Bull Island on the tenth has continued. I went for a late high-tide sail yesterday, sailing through the wide creeks and sections of marsh flooded by the tide. There is the promise of the continued southwest sea breeze filling in as the day warms up. I am underway a little after noon and reach out though Anderson Creek. Compared to the high tide of the previous evening, the creeks are like gorges today. *Kingfisher* is now planing across the bay in optimum conditions for a fast passage to the Northeast Point. *Kingfisher* touches the sand about thirty-five minutes after leaving the dock. It is an incredible low tide, the lowest I have ever seen here. I must combine my long mooring line to my main sheet to reach the snag to tie off.

My plan is to hike along up to the entrance to the dike and road system I accessed last in April. I will stay on the eastern side of Jacks Creek, go past the entrance to the Boneyard, walk farther on the beach looking for turtle crawls, and loop back down the beach. For my return sail I am considering sailing off to Marsh Island, a rookery island located in the middle of the bay. I begin my walk looking at the sand flats exposed by low tide. Numerous species usually concealed are now beached in the sun including sea slugs, starfish and horseshoe crabs.

I recall a June night of my pre-adolescence growing up in New Jersey. I was staying with a friend, and we went out on a full-moon night in his neighborhood. We walked down to the Navesink River and encountered an amazing scene. Hundreds of horseshoe crabs were coming up on a little beach in the light of the full moon, and some rode on top of others. For more than three hundred million years this ancient orgy has occurred on the full-moon high tides of summer, and we were witness to this awesome event. Unfortunately the wonder of being present for the spawning of horseshoe crabs was lost on us; instead I followed the others in an act of adolescent ignorance by smashing one horseshoe crab with another, and impaling the sharp tail of one crab into another. The memory of that summer night is still mingled with awe and guilt.

Horseshoe crabs existed before the evolution of birds or fish, and they have been treated for years as worthless and in some cases harmful predators of shellfish. Commercial uses have included fertilizer or bait for eel and conch fishermen. In more recent years science has discovered new value from these ancient animals. The blood of horseshoe crabs was found to be the raw material needed for the production of a test for the deadly gram-negative bacteria, responsible for diseases such as *E. coli*, Legionnaire's disease and meningitis. A multimillion-dollar industry has learned to "bleed" the horseshoe crabs to produce Limulus lysate, the substance used to test for endotoxins. A Charleston-based company, Endosafe, accesses the local horseshoe crab population, and after the extraction returns the crabs to their marine environment. A second discovery from ornithological research has disclosed that a number of shorebirds migrating on the Atlantic Flyway, including several species of sandpipers and plovers that visit the Cape Romain NWR, are dependent on horseshoe-crab eggs for their long journey from South America to their Arctic breeding grounds. The shorebird feeding on horseshoe-crab eggs is just one example of how these ancient but highly adapted animals fit into the web of life.

Preparing to enter the dike and road system in the same place I did in April, I find an unusual barrier in the way. The sand area before the high dunes has numerous signs indicating a "Closed Area." Further information is given on these signs; the area is being used to help conserve seabeach amaranth, an endangered plant. This annual helps to provide some of the early stabilization of sand required for dune formation. It has become threatened, along with many other plant and animal species, due to coastal development. The historic range of seabeach amaranth is from Cape Cod to Kiawah Island, and due to its disappearance in two-thirds of this range, the plant was added to the national list of endangered and threatened species. This conservation project by the U.S. Fish and Wildlife Service includes the propagation of plants by seed in a greenhouse at Oak Island, North Carolina, and the transplanting of the young plants to several locations in South Carolina, including the north and south ends of Bull Island. Hurricane Hugo decimated the Bull Island population of this plant down to 188 plants in 1990. The conservation project, initiated in 2000, showed promising results; a survey in 2004 found over 1,100 plants on Bull Island, and many of these plants have germinated on their own from seed.

This recovery site for seabeach amaranth is symbolic of one component of the mission of the entire National Wildlife Refuge System—the protection and recovery of endangered and threatened species. The refuge system is administered by the U.S. Fish and Wildlife Service, and included in the agency's responsibilities is the endangered species program. This year marks the hundredth anniversary of the creation of the national program in 1903 by President Theodore Roosevelt. He saw a need to protect diminishing and disappearing species when he wrote, "To lose the chance to see frigate-birds soaring in circles above the storm, or a file of pelicans winging their way homeward across the crimson afterglow of the sunset, or a myriad terns flashing in the bright light of midday as they hover in a shifting maze above the beach—why, the loss is like the loss of a gallery of the masterpieces of the artists of old time." Cape Romain is but one of 540 refuges in the United States. Charismatic species such as loggerhead turtles and red wolves have received a lion's share of the attention, but there is obviously much other work going on to conserve species and ecosystems. The modest seabeach amaranth is a good example of this effort. There have been successes, such as the bald eagle, which moved from endangered to threatened on the federal endangered species list, and now is recommended for de-listing. However, the number of species added to the list each year averages eighty-five. Bull Island and the entire Cape Romain NWR are important biological holdings for our community and the greater natural world.

Deciding to err on the side of safety and not trespass in this restricted area, I instead walk up the beach past the first shallow inlet and toward the next access to the road system. Only a few flies nag on the short walk into the vegetation on the sides of the dike, and once on top, the fine sea breeze dispels all comers and precludes the need for repellant. Encountered on the top of the dike is a pair of black-necked stilts, and I wonder if they are the same pair I observed earlier in the week on the dunes. They display the protective characteristics of nesting shorebirds and both cry out at me, making several diving threats toward my head. I get the message and move on down the dike. On top of this dike, elevated considerably for storm protection, a beautiful panorama unfolds: ocean and beach to the left and the freshwater environment of the Jacks Creek impoundment to the right. Without much searching, an array of wading birds and alligators comes into focus.

I follow the road system to the east and then one of the several trails spilling out on the Boneyard. It is time for a swim and lunch sitting on the sand amongst the trees by the water. Some footprints besides mine are on the beach and I note these novel tracks. A real human encounter occurs when a Cape Romain NWR four-wheeler comes from the south on the beach. Speaking to a Cape Romain NWR staffer, I learn that they have been looking for turtle crawls and have only seen one false crawl. They are carrying a derelict crab trap on the rear of their vehicle, and I describe the location of another seen earlier. They head that way as I finish lunch. Since they have already surveyed the beach I planned to walk to search for turtle signs, I grab my stuff for the walk back to the Northeast Point. I pick my way through the trees strewn out over the beach and appreciate the refuge staffers' ability to find a path through here for the four-wheeler. The vehicle is soon coming my way carrying the second crab pot I had described. The staff person stops to tell me he noticed a false crawl up the beach and marked it with the swerve of his vehicle. At these marks, clear flipper scrapes indicate the large animal dragging up the beach and then back to the ocean. Some combination of observations and instincts told the turtle that this was not the right place to nest.

Of the wildlife conservation programs associated with the Cape Romain NWR, perhaps none is more prominent than the loggerhead turtle program. The refuge provides the largest nesting area for the Atlantic loggerhead sea turtle north of Florida. Due to predation and beach erosion, a management program to increase the rate of hatchling survival has been ongoing; a main task has been to relocate eggs from nests into a protective hatchery. This program takes place on North Cape Island, the most northerly of the refuge islands. An aerial survey of crawls takes place annually on Bull Island, and 180 nests were identified by this survey in 2003, producing close to a thousand hatchlings. Over 1,000 nests were counted on North and South Cape Islands in the same year and the North Cape hatcheries produced about fifty-two thousand hatchlings.

The life cycle of sea turtles has come to light due to the research efforts of biologists. Just years ago there was little information as to where the turtle hatchlings went after hitting the surf—they just seemed to disappear. We now know they take off on a thirty-six-hour swimming frenzy to the Gulf Stream, where they reside in the Sargasso Sea eating sargassum, crabs and jellyfish. A research project, the Satellite Telemetry Study, has been underway for the past few years. Transmitters are attached to the shells of loggerheads after they lay their eggs on Cape Island. Researchers follow the turtles by satellite tracking, and the public can also track the turtles' movements via web pages. One of the conclusions of this study is that the refuge loggerheads are mainly spending their time away from here in the waters north to New Jersey.

Researchers have been working hard to understand many of the mysteries of this unique group of animals. How do the hatchlings know where to go after hatching and digging out of the sand? Where do they go and how do they find their way back? What are the navigation mechanisms of loggerheads, a sea animal that only spends 5 percent of its time on the surface? Researchers have found that sea turtle navigation is multifaceted, using celestial and magnetic clues as well as swell refraction. While the answers are finally becoming known, our wonder for the sophistication and capability of this animal grows, as do conservation efforts.

I push on toward the north and still see footprints along the high-tide line. I almost miss the Waiting Beach, and although pelicans are absent today there is an array of terns, oystercatchers and black skimmers. The skimmers are in an interesting and comical pose—they are lying prone on their chests. The predicted dark clouds and growing thunderheads make their presence known over the mainland, and I quicken my pace as I note the incoming tide between the two shallow inlets. I now encounter others on the beach and see a college-age man walking ahead of a group of teenage girls and their mother. He asks me how far to the Boneyard, and I share with him information about the false turtle crawl. Before I turn the point, a man standing watch over a boat at the inlet asks about the group of four I encountered. They have made the trip up from the Isle of Palms, and he too is keeping an eye on the mainland weather.

I arrive back at *Kingfisher*, and after finishing lunch I rig for sailing and ponder the weather. Like the turtle that made the false crawl, my head and instincts tell me today is not right for the trip to Marsh Island due to the late hour, the threat of thunderstorms and a long return beat to windward. Instead, I set a course across the bay to pass close to the southern end of Bird Island, the shoal I had seen in the distance in May. These are fairly uncharted waters for me, though I sailed across and bumped into the bay shoals in the past in my Hobie 16. It is two hours after the very low tide, and the rising tide is an important asset as I reach into these shoal waters. Despite that good news, in the reach across to the island the daggerboard hits bottom several times. Closing on Bird Island, the light chop of the bay breaks ahead signaling even shallower waters. These disturbances and instinct lead me to pass the island—a sandy shoal with no vegetation. Birds are hanging out on the isle's tip, brown pelicans and the other usual suspects. *Kingfisher* is passing through, but I look over to the isle and wonder if there is a deeper channel running by it. I jibe and reach over, and not only must I pull up the daggerboard farther but the rudder is popped up in the shallow water. With maneuvering options exhausted I step out into the water to physically turn *Kingfisher* around. Clumps of grass are scattered across the sandy bottom. It is clear that this little shoal is underwater on very high tides. In past years this island had a strip of small sand dunes down its center and was an important colonial nesting island. As the island changed, it was finally abandoned for nesting, as survival instincts led birds elsewhere.

Kingfisher and I search for deeper water while reaching off the shoal, and once found, I sheet in and head up for my best guess at the location of the mouth of Venning Creek. I have never approached this creek from the current course, and a sandy area on the bay's edge is a main reference point to me since the creek mouth lies to the north of the reference. Seeing boats farther to the south in the bay I begin to wonder as I grow closer, but I spot what looks like a marker, a piece of galvanized pipe pushed into the bottom. I bear off and after getting close to the marsh I see the opening. The creek grasps *Kingfisher* in its greenness in the reach through the smooth waters. A turn to the southwest in this creek brings *Kingfisher* back to beating to windward and making use of all the available water in the creek. This is great practice in tacking the boat efficiently, maintaining movement and sailing the boat as close to the wind as possible. One tack is held too long and the daggerboard crunches into a submerged oyster bar. After passing through the little narrow sound behind the Intracoastal Waterway shell banks, *Kingfisher* enters into the waterway for the final beat to the landing. The simple task becomes comic: when using my feet to tend sail while my hands are adjusting the chin strap of my hat, the sheet slips, spilling the wind and heeling *Kingfisher* sharply to windward. I receive a wet butt in this unceremonious approach to the landing.

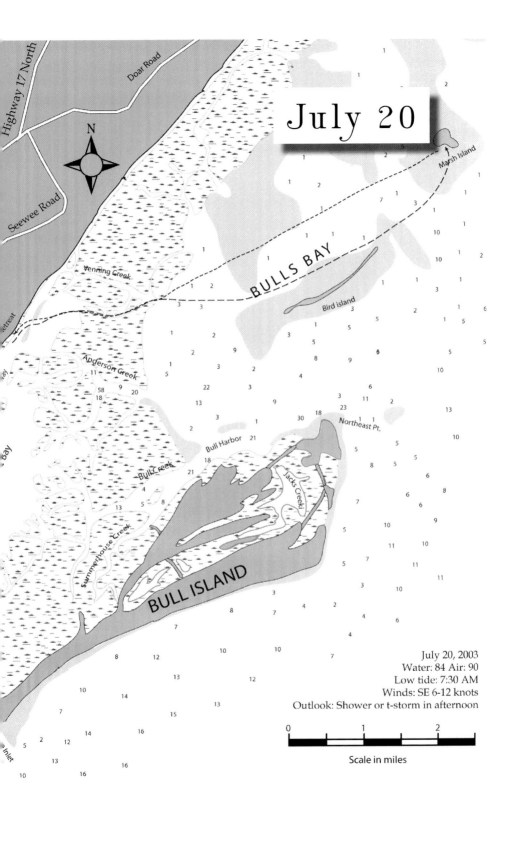

July 20

Highway 17 North

Doar Road

N

Seewee Road

Marsh Island

BULLS BAY

Venning Creek

Bird Island

Anderson Creek

Bull Harbor

Northeast Pt.

Bull Creek

Jacks Creek

Bay

Summerhouse Creek

BULL ISLAND

Inlet

July 20, 2003
Water: 84 Air: 90
Low tide: 7:30 AM
Winds: SE 6-12 knots
Outlook: Shower or t-storm in afternoon

0   1   2

Scale in miles

I dropped *Kingfisher* in earlier this morning and now return to the landing by bike to find her floating and ready to raise sail. There are numerous dragonflies and my potential crew, greenhead flies, in the air. I push off into the waterway, raise sail and am off at eleven o'clock. The breeze is variable and a light zephyr is off of the land. I ghost across the waterway, but as I try to run through a little channel between shell banks am stopped by the incoming tide. I do not have my usual aid of the outgoing tide to make it out to the bay, so I will look to auxiliary power. I rig my tiller extension and begin to paddle. I have a new goal in my sights: with the predicted southeast wind I plan to head north into Bulls Bay via Venning Creek and make my way across the bay to Marsh Island, a tiny isolated isle that at present is a location of colonial seabird nesting in the refuge. This voyage will take me into new waters heading north from Bull Island.

I have chosen to head out Venning Creek since it will put me farther into the bay than my usual outlet, Anderson Creek. I decide to take a secondary waterway through the marsh parallel to the main Venning channel. I am finding virtually no breeze so I get into a paddling rhythm, recalling my past canoeing days. I find this secondary channel has less incoming flow than the main Venning Creek, and my progress is better than anticipated. I hug the marsh grass at the edge of the creek and note on the chart that this course is actually a bit shorter than the main Venning course. Several large oyster bars dot this creek that parallels a third channel of the same size. Occasionally a little breeze adds to the push, but it is mainly paddling that gets me to a northern bend in the creek. From my vantage point I can see far in the distance the outlet to Bulls Bay that appears calm and glassy. At 11:45 my sail is suddenly shifted from starboard to port by a real puff from the southeast, and this seems a clear sign of the arrival of the sea breeze. I recall the most noticed and appreciated arrival of the sea breeze in all my days of sailing. Prior to my return to graduate school I sensed a shift in my life, and wanted one last adventure. My friend and kindred spirit Rusty Davies and I headed north out of Masonboro Inlet at Wrightsville Beach on my Hobie 16. Our final goal was the Outer Banks, and we planned to camp along the way. Our progress was initially slow as we hoped and prayed for the regular breeze to arise; the filling in of that sea breeze was a joyful experience as we began our adventure-filled voyage. Today there are several holes in this new breeze in the creek, but the paddle and tiller extension are stowed as I see that the bay is currently filled with wind. I still have to encounter the strong flow of incoming tide at the mouth of the creek but after one tack I am easily out, closehauled on the starboard tack, and heading on the long axis of the bay to the northeast.

The bay is all mine without another boat in sight, and using my chart and the few landmarks available I steer for the unseen island. The sailing is very smooth since this southeast sea breeze is light but steady and the water has little chop. Occasionally the ease and relaxation of this sail is interrupted by a bite from one of my greenhead crew, probing such unusual bite areas as the back of the foot. I plan to skirt Bird Island shoal, which in the past has been a prime colonial nesting island. I soon sight this shoal and decide to take a tack closer. After a short hitch I tack back to my previous course to the northeast. I am close enough to see brown pelicans hanging out where I saw them on my last sail. Perhaps in an accreted future this island will rise to its former status as bird rookery. Past this shoal my daggerboard finds an extension of the shallow bottom, requiring me to pull it up to the halfway point to decrease my draft. That seems to do fine as I continue to sail over these shallow smooth waters with the steady breeze.

Marsh Island is still not visible, and I begin to wonder about my bearing. Yet my worries are trivial. The breeze is fair, and the return voyage will be an easy reach compared to the long beat to windward usually required by a southwest breeze. Additionally, the tide is coming in so I have more freedom to move over the shallow waters. The shoals off to the east display the surf of the outside swells breaking on them. Beyond these eastern shoals appear markers for the entrance to Five Fathom Creek, the channel that leads from the ocean to McClellanville.

With the aid of binoculars I identify boats fishing on the outer shoals that mark the beginning of Bulls Bay, and shrimpers outside of the marked channel. But there is still no sign of Marsh Island. Considering the prodigious navigation feats of migrating birds and sea turtles, my minor navigation challenge is a humbling experience.

Changing the bearing of *Kingfisher*, I finally pick out an island in the distance with definite marsh areas and conclude this land is my objective. My bearing now is farther away from the east, more toward the north on a broad reach, so I am making an arc across the bay in search of Marsh Island. Although the southeast wind continues to push *Kingfisher* ahead, the island only appears close in the binoculars. Drawing closer I see that the island is composed of sections of marsh and vegetated high ground. A sandy beach is nestled in a thickly vegetated area, and *Kingfisher* assumes this heading. Terns in flight between Marsh and Bull Islands confirm my course. A boat appears in the distance heading toward me in the bay, passing by Marsh Island and rounding on my side. He redoubles his course and heads east on the other side of Marsh Island toward Raccoon Key and the north Cape Romain NWR islands.

Ahead, a shoal is marked by the break of the small swell. The best course appears through these little breakers. *Kingfisher* makes it through the small break without splashing the skipper, and as I now close with the island the impact of the life ahead hits me. Thousands of birds are covering the island and wheeling in the air all around. It seems like the beach area is completely filled with birds of various species including pelicans, terns and gulls. The air is filled with tightly circling birds, and the powerful visual stimulus is matched by the sonic cacophony of squawks, screeches, laughs, peeps and other bird sounds. Entry onto Marsh Island is prohibited at this time of year, so I tack before I get to the beach, letting my sail luff and the boat drift. I stand up in *Kingfisher*'s cockpit and observe with the binoculars. Several "Closed Area" signs are posted in the midst of the wildness, but the chaotic display is enough to keep me off this place. Part of the survival strategy of birds on these colonial nesting islands is strength in numbers, and they will dive, mob, peck and defecate on potential predators, including humans. Beyond this part of the island, there is nesting activity everywhere. The island is covered with bird life and obviously the isolated location out in this shallow bay has ensured reduced predation, especially from the main thief of nesting colonies, the raccoon. I have seen nesting before on barrier islands but nothing has prepared me for this scene. The anticipation of making this trip, of finding this wild place, and of experiencing this nursery for so many birds is magnificent.

Marsh Island in Bulls Bay is a mecca for birds that return here to nest and for young birds returning to their birthplace. Birds invite our interest and wonder in many ways, but contemplation of one of the cornerstones of bird survival, migration, provokes our fascination. In past decades researchers have begun to unravel this mystery. A biological rationale for migration is the need for bird species to travel to optimum conditions for reproduction and survival. We know where birds go when they leave us; their pathways cross small and large areas of the earth, and in the case of the Arctic tern the passage is Arctic to Antarctic. The means of navigating for birds is multifaceted, including the sun (an internal sundial), sensitivity to ultraviolet radiation, sensitivity to earth's magnetic field and celestial navigation for night flying. Birds appear to have a "cerebral compass." These capacities are built-in, and as the documentary filmmaker of *Winged Migration* Jacques Perrin stated, "In the egg, they already know the entry codes to the great secrets of the machinery of the universe."

Some of the most spectacular of the globetrotting migrants are the terns. These are most distinctive seabirds known to some as sea swallows. Two of the groups with significant nesting numbers on Marsh Island are the royal and sandwich terns. In 2003, according to Cape Romain NWR biologist Sarah Dawsey, nest totals for royal and sandwich terns were 979 and 89, respectively, with dramatic increases in 2004 (2,467 and 586). Of their many attributes is a skill in fishing, which ranks high and includes the ability to hover before diving into water. The sandwich terns may fly thirty to forty miles offshore on their fishing trips. Royal terns feed their young for a lengthy term (up to seven months) before the young birds have developed the competency to fish for their survival. The banding of royals occurred for the first time in the refuge in 2004. But we still have much to learn from these birds that traverse the globe through the domains of sky, water and earth.

One of the terns flying under my radar and nesting to the northeast on Cape Island is the least tern. This smallest of the South Carolina terns has a wing beat so fast that the beats often cannot be counted. Like other terns, the least is a globetrotter covering thousands of miles in its migration; many of these birds winter in South America. With the decline of many of the plume bird species toward the end of the nineteenth century, the least tern was also hunted for its feathers for women's hats. The noted South Carolina ornithologist Arthur T. Wayne observed in 1910 that northern hunters had shot all the nesting least terns on Bull Island, and at one point he felt this bird had become extinct on the coast. The species did face extinction but conservation efforts helped the population recover. Least tern numbers are again diminished due to human pressure, and the species is listed as threatened in South Carolina. The nesting site in the refuge is the largest in the state.

Finally ready to leave, I stow my binoculars, pull out my lunch and sheet in my sail to head home. The wind remains steady and I secure sail and tiller so I can eat lunch while cruising on. My return course should cut time off the passage to Marsh Island and will keep me closer to the mainland or western side of the bay. The bay is still separated from the mainland by salt marsh and the Intracoastal Waterway, and this area of marsh has only a few creek systems that connect the waterway with the bay. On my present course I find some homemade markers ahead warning of shoals. One of these shoals is a small sand mound high and dry and covered with pelicans. A large open shed built on pilings once stood in this area of Bulls Bay. It was an oyster factory owned and operated by the Magwood family, who lived on Bull Island in the nineteenth and early twentieth centuries. Built into this shed was a dormitory for the workers who shucked the oysters for packing and shipping to market. This business included the harvesting of clams and the catching of diamondback terrapins that were shipped to northern markets.

It is high tide now, and far ahead the area of marsh between Bull Island and the Intracoastal appears mainly underwater. From this perspective Bull Island appears more isolated and mysterious. I expect an easier time finding the mouth to Venning Creek, but I still have to close this distance. A second boat makes an appearance coming from the south end of the bay. It follows my wake in the opposite direction and disappears to the west of Marsh Island. I recall my difficulty finding Venning Creek on my last voyage due to the hiding of the opening as one approaches from the south. I noted the landmarks this morning as I left, with the western marsh of the bay containing a sandy area about a third of a mile to the south of the creek mouth, and a scalloped cove from the sandy area to the creek. These landmarks finally appear clearly, and the banks of the mouth are fairly underwater. *Kingfisher* sails in easily and returns into the southernmost creek. I transition to the green serenity of the estuarine salt marsh, sailing easily and freely. The hush of the marsh is broken by not just one but three motorboats roaring by in this narrow waterway, and *Kingfisher* hugs the marsh bank as I wave to this convoy. Soon the outboard sounds dissipate in the marsh, and *Kingfisher* returns to a solo passage. One of the oyster bars ahead has an assemblage of birds, including an American oystercatcher, a cormorant and a large group of "peeps." These sandpipers take to the air, break into two groups, and wheel as two separate entities. I arrive at the

Intracoastal Waterway, and while coming through the channel between the shell banks I make a hard impact, stopping *Kingfisher* dead in the water until I raise the daggerboard. My running aground on this shell bank, covered by the high tide, embeds part of an oyster shell in the foot of the board, as I find on later inspection. I complete the final reach across the waterway, round to the wind, drop sail and paddle to the dock for the landing. The favorable conditions today provided me the opportunity to explore almost to the far end of the bay, and an isolated island providing the protection for a major rookery. I had not seen this colonial nesting island until today, and I dream of the other islands to the north I have yet to see and explore.

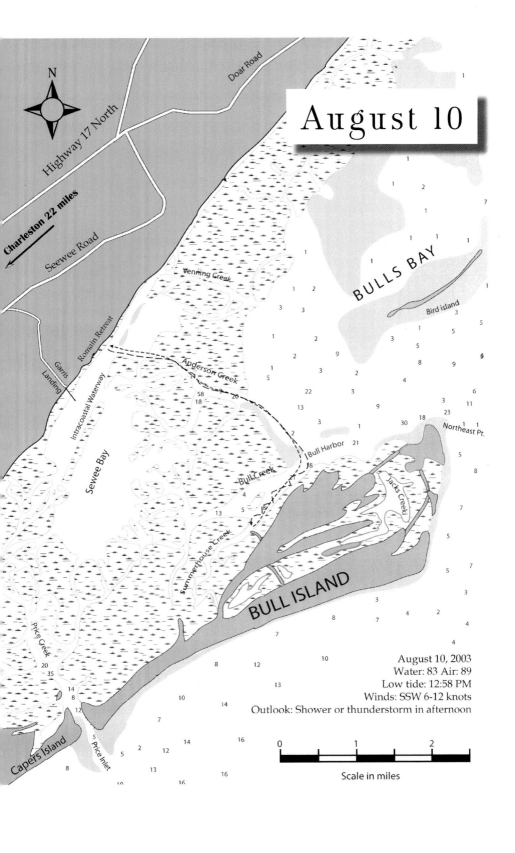

August 10

August 10, 2003
Water: 83 Air: 89
Low tide: 12:58 PM
Winds: SSW 6-12 knots
Outlook: Shower or thunderstorm in afternoon

Scale in miles

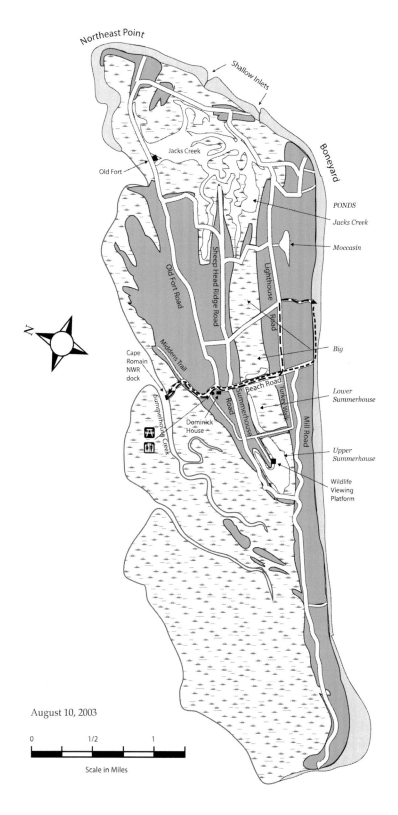

Northeast Point

Shallow Inlets

Jacks Creek

Old Fort

Boneyard

PONDS

Jacks Creek

Moccasin

Old Fort Road

Sheep Head Ridge Road

Lighthouse Road

Big

N

Cape Romain NWR dock

Middens Trail

Beach Road

Turkey Walk

Lower Summerhouse

Summerhouse Creek

Summerhouse Road

Mill Road

Dominick House

Upper Summerhouse

Wildlife Viewing Platform

ATLANTIC OCEAN

August 10, 2003

0   1/2   1

Scale in Miles

My anticipation for heading out to the island today is tempered with the memory of my last attempt to sail out in late July. Caution kept me on shore that day, watching the battle between the sea breeze and the local weather system over the mainland that continued to build and darken. Slowly, inexorably the thunderstorm system won out, and I realized I would be paddling into a dying sea breeze and incoming tide with an imminent thunderstorm perhaps bearing down. But could I get out to the sea breeze and maybe stay out of harm's way? The pull was powerful, much like the seabirds heading back to Marsh Island to nest, and the loggerheads finding their way back to North Cape Island. At that critical moment a kingfisher appeared overhead, hovering with rapid wing beat, and the shrill sound emanating from this bird seemed a strident warning. I heeded this sign, and let go of my need to set sail and set foot on the island that day.

This morning a beautiful south-southwest breeze blows away any remaining apprehension. The strong outgoing tide with the breeze carries me quickly through the curves of Anderson Creek, and I pass numerous herons, egrets and patrolling pelicans. From the mouth of Anderson Creek the reach across the bay is brisk, and the Northeast Point would be an easy course. But today I plan to set off on a walk from the refuge dock across the island to the central beach. I therefore must pass the shallow water shoaling out from the bay's bank before I make the turn into Bull Creek, where I will face both an opposing wind direction and outgoing tide. My attempt at cheating a little around the corner fails when I run aground and I must continue on until I make Bull Creek. This course will challenge my skills going to windward against the tidal flow. I see a boat ahead anchored on the Bull Island side of the creek, and three men have this area all to themselves as I enter. I avoid disturbing them by tacking away and then back to the island. I must focus on playing the wind shifts and stay on the island side of the creek to look for a slower tidal flow. Occasionally it is "up daggerboard" as I play the creek side too tightly. As I leave the three fishermen astern they appear idyllically framed in the beautiful clear air: their silhouettes on the protected creek waters, the soothing green of the adjacent marsh and the sublime backdrop of the sparkling waters of Bulls Bay reaching to the horizon and meeting the stunning blue sky.

Farther on up the creek I find some advantage from the bend of Bull Creek to the west, and the tidal flow now pushes my bow in a favorable direction. My course now takes me into Summerhouse Creek, and due to my windward zigzag course I notice how narrow this creek is. Since I am so close to the island the wind coming through is more variable in strength and direction. Suddenly a radical wind shift backs my sail; my slow reaction has the windward rail underwater along with my butt, and I face a potential capsize to windward. I hang on and finally come back to normal trim. As I land I notice that there are no boats at the floating dock, and the ferry *Island Cat* is not here. I am surprised on such a beautiful Sunday that I have the dock area to myself. I go about securing *Kingfisher*. A premature start of the walk requires me to return to the boat to grab my bug spray in anticipation of biting insects. I put on long sleeves before I set out, just before noon. There are only refuge vehicle tire tracks and no footprints on the road. Past the open picnic area is Dominick House. The building, now quarters for refuge staff, survived Hurricane Hugo. According to Larry Davis of Cape Romain NWR, a small corridor of the island in this location appeared to have been spared the extreme devastation elsewhere, and a nearby kiosk also came through intact. The house had been clad a few years before Hugo with vinyl siding and only one piece came off. There was a little roof damage, but the storm surge left mud throughout the ground floor, a calling card from Hugo. The vinyl siding is gone now and the exterior is certainly in need of maintenance. Window air conditioner units disturb the lines of the building and some of the siding shingles are missing. It is sad that the island's only historic building that weathered ground zero of the massive storm is now suffering from neglect.

Beach Road runs across the dike between Big Pond and the Lower Summerhouse Pond. The water level is quite low and several small alligators leave a trail of brownish scum as they swim along in a little channel. Everywhere there is the new green growth of colonizing plants. At the intersection of Beach and Lighthouse Roads I turn left, planning to walk north down the Lighthouse Road, take the first trail to the beach and loop back down to the Beach Road. Butterflies and dragonflies reign in the air, and there are fewer mosquitoes than anticipated. There is water close to the road in many places. First one plop and then many signal a troop of small frogs. It is not far to the trail heading to the beach, and this narrow path passes over a wetland. This wetland area changes quickly with the elevation of a large former dune and the transition to pines, palmettos and live oaks in beautiful resurgence of the maritime forest. There is actually a little climb up the first elevation, and then up and down several times until the sandy path leads into the sculpted shapes of oak, yaupon and myrtle and a wide area of dunes before the primary dunes. There is a fairly high primary dune scarp that has been carved by the ocean at storm tides. There are no human footprints but other prints abound including ghost crab and deer. I strip down to bathing suit and cool off in the ocean. There is an impressive width of beach on this low tide—about 150 yards of hard sand from water's edge to the dune scarp.

After lunch I take a look again at the area between the primary dunes and the sculpted edge of the maritime forest. Arrayed throughout this transition area are the dead remains of live oak trees still jutting up through the new growth. Terns fly by, and I have a new outlook on these marvelous birds after my visit to their nesting colony in July. There are no other people on the beach in either direction. I collect my gear and head south toward the main path to Beach Road. At first glance the shells at the high-tide line are not spectacular, and most abundant is the ark shell. I estimate the length of time to get to the entrance to the Beach Road, and my timing is right on. But I still get there too soon, and wandering a little bit farther I realize that I am not ready for the beach part of the walk to be over. I find a log to sit on for some moments of contemplation. At the entrance to the dune path a different viewpoint allows for further contemplation of the ocean, sky, dunes and maritime forest.

The integrated zones of beach, dunes, shrub community and maritime forest are a complex system. A defining factor is the proximity to the ocean, with salt spray from ocean breezes being a keen pruning tool in nature's hand. Pines rising up through the canopy on the front line of salt exposure have turned brown. The live oak trees of the canopy are resistant to salt spray and provide protection for understory trees to thrive, and in turn stabilize the soil. As noted before this elegant system of different plant communities has been roughly hewn by the ocean on the eastern side of the island, and will continue to be rudely affected by storms and the rising sea level more radically than elsewhere on the shoreline.

Proceeding down the Beach Road I remember the big gator from March, and I peer under the branches at his dark pool of water. Despite searching from several angles, there is no sign of him. Looking across the ponds ahead there is a clear man-made straight line on this road and dike for over half a mile, all the way to the clearing by Dominick House. There is the glint of a refuge vehicle windshield in this direction, and it turns off to the south on Summerhouse Road. But no one is encountered before I reach Dominick House. In front of the house stands a grove of prominent live oaks. They, like the house itself, are survivors of Hurricane Hugo. Though these trees bear some signs of the ravage of that great storm, they have recovered their eminence. The renowned naturalist John Muir described the live oak as "the most magnificent planted tree that I have ever seen." John Lawson, in *A New Voyage to Carolina*, also commented on the appearance of two trees planted from the acorns by Indians, saying he "never saw anything more beautiful of that kind." Lawson also mentioned that these trees were found on dry, sandy "Knolls," and Bull Island's sandy ridges provided the hummocks, a perfect setting for the oaks' natural cultivation. The entire island was most likely once covered with fine mature live oaks. The timber of these trees that grow throughout the southeast United States was recognized in the colonial period for its superiority as a shipbuilding wood. The wood is very heavy, dense and durable, and distinctively resistant to splitting and rot. While not good timber for the straight pieces needed for keels, spars and planking, the natural curves of the tree were well suited for creating the curved frames required for wooden ships. This June I lent a hand (in a ceremonial sort of way) to the erecting of several live oak frames for the twenty-first-century construction of a vessel whose lines were taken from a nineteenth-century pilot schooner, the *Frances Elizabeth*. She was named after the wife of the Charleston shipbuilder Samuel Pregnall, who at one time was part owner of Bull Island. The new vessel, the *Spirit of South Carolina*, has a backbone built from live oaks removed from Lowcountry roadways. Downed live oaks from Hurricane Hugo were also utilized for the renovation of USS *Constitution*.

In 1799 the U.S. Navy approved the construction of six 74-gun ships-of-the-line. These large warships required large amounts of timber, and the framework for one would consume 680 mature live oak trees. At the time, the owner of Bull Island was Colonel Thomas Shubrick, and he was awarded a contract with the navy to provide the live oak timber for two of the planned gun ships. The scale of this operation was so immense and difficult that Shubrick and another contractor, Phineas Miller of Cumberland Island, Georgia, corresponded on the unanticipated and considerable difficulties. Miller, in a letter to Shubrick, commented, "The further I advance in this purplexing contract for Timber, the greater do I find the difficulty the expense & the disappointment." Shubrick was to find similar troubles. There was not enough skilled labor in Charleston for this job, so Shubrick hired sixty-five ship carpenters from Newburyport, Massachusetts. Bringing these Yankees to South Carolina was not an isolated enterprise, for the Massachusetts men, reared in northern shipbuilding communities, soon began making an annual journey south for work known as "live oaking." This job required not just the felling of timber, but also the shaping of each specific timber to exact dimensions provided by a mold or pattern of the actual frame. According to the contract, the timber should "not exceed the Mould by more than one Inch in Breadth, Thickness or Length," and this requirement reduced the extra costs of freighting the timber to northern shipyards. Slave labor was also utilized, as elsewhere in this industry in the southeast, and Shubrick leased an additional forty local slaves as carpenters.

It is hard to imagine the physical labor required to fell, hew, carry and stow this timber in the transport vessels. Lawson noted that the wood "frightens our Sawyers from the Fatigue that attends the cutting of this Timber." Most of the felling and shaping of the timber was performed by ax. Another famed naturalist, John James Audubon, observed the felling of huge live oaks on a hummock in Florida. His eyewitness account gives us insight into the process:

> *I think I see them proceeding to their work. Here two have stationed themselves on the opposite sides of the trunk of a noble and venerable live-oak. Their keen-edged and well-tempered axes seem to make no impression on it, so small are the chips that drop at each blow around the mossy and wide-spreading roots. There, one is*

ascending the stem of another, of which, in its fall, the arms have stuck among the tangled tops of the neighboring trees. See how cautiously he proceeds, barefooted, and with a handkerchief around his head. Now he has climbed to the height of about forty feet from the ground; he stops, and squaring himself with the trunk on which he so boldly stands, he wields with sinewy arms his trusty blade, the repeated blows of which, although the tree be as tough as it is large, will soon sever it in two. He has changed sides, and his back is turned to you. The trunk now remains connected by only a thin strip of wood. He places his feet on the part which is lodged, and shakes it with all his might. Now swings the huge log under his leaps, now it suddenly gives way, and as it strikes upon the ground its echoes are repeated through the hummock, and every Wild Turkey within hearing utters his gobble of recognition. The wood-cutter, however, remains collected and composed; but the next moment, he throws his axe to the ground, and, assisted by the nearest grape-vine, slides down and reaches the earth in an instant.

Hewing the timbers to the exacting dimensions was a much more skilled task than felling the trees, and Phineas Miller noted that out of his thirty-six workmen only two had the necessary skills to mold the timber precisely. After the fallen timber was pronounced sound, the hewer would score lines and square off the timber using the felling ax, and then hewing to the line with a broadax. The molds were used to score the exact pattern of the timber, whether a futtock (frame), a knee, a floor timber or other frame member.

Moving these extremely heavy timbers to the landing required an ancient device, the timber cart, or big wheels. A single axle connected the pair of wooden wheels with a diameter of seven to twelve feet, and iron tires. The carts had to carry the timbers not on firm roads but through swampy areas, thick vegetation and rough, sandy trails and roads. A single man, the teamster, was able to load the huge green live oak "stick" using the other parts of the cart: a wooden bed and pole over the axle, a tongue and chains. But the living component of this hauling practice was the Yankee live oakers' favorite beast of burden—oxen. These animals were instrumental in getting the timber out of the forest and to the landing, and possessed a combination of strength, fine disposition and immunity to the distractions provided by the abundant wildlife of the maritime forest. Once at the landing, probably near the present refuge dock on Bull Island, the timber was loaded onto shallow draft lighters or scows. The timber would then be moved to the transport vessels, mostly likely schooners. An act passed in 1799 specified that the ships be 150 tons burthen and draw no more than twelve feet when loaded. These vessels would have had to navigate the shoals of Bull Inlet before the ocean voyage to their northern destination.

The men who performed this grueling labor would have set up camp on the island first by constructing palmetto-roofed shacks. Shubrick paid for the round-trip transport of the Newburyport live oakers and was also responsible for their board. During this period of work on the island, five of the Massachusetts carpenters died. All told, the enterprise was a financial failure for Shubrick, and he was only able to produce timber for two-thirds of the frames of one ship. Many of the mature trees were found to have rot developing from the heart of the tree, and this was only discovered after the tree was cut down. In correspondence with Navy Secretary Benjamin Stoddert, Shubrick described the report by his foreman of ten trees cut down and six being so defective as to not produce a single timber. He mentioned one particular live oak, with a girth of 24 feet, which had been slated to produce the main transom timber. This tree also proved to be "defective." It is relevant to note that the Angel Oak, considered the largest and oldest live oak tree existing today (over twelve hundred years old), has a girth of 25 ½ feet.

Shubrick ended up losing money on his contract; it was estimated he received $17,000 and spent $22,000. A good portion of the 1,050 pieces of live oak timber still lay on the ground years later. A court case after Shubrick's death in 1810 involved his heirs, creditors and the government. His son Edward Shubrick continued to petition the government in 1825 for funds from that 1799 contract.

Despite Thomas Shubrick's shortfall in providing timbers for two 74-gun ships, the Shubricks made other contributions to the U.S. Navy. Shubrick and his wife Mary Branford had fifteen children, eleven that survived into adulthood. Four of the sons born on Bull Island had careers in the U.S. Navy. Edward Rutledge Shubrick (named for his uncle, a signer of the Declaration of Independence) was warranted as a midshipman in 1807, promoted to commodore in 1828, and captain in 1831. He commanded the *Vincennes* of the India squadron and later the *Columbia* of the Brazilian squadron. He died at sea in 1844. A second brother, Irvine Templer, was a midshipman in service with his brother, Lieutenant John Templer Shubrick. The British captured their ship, *President*, and they were carried to Bermuda where they were held as prisoners of war. Irvine also became a commander in 1841 and commanded *Saratoga* on the Brazil station. John Templer had an active naval career; notable when, as lieutenant on *Constitution*, he commanded the quarter-deck guns in the capture of *Guerriere*. He served as first lieutenant of the *Guerriere* under Captain Stephen Decatur and after the capture of the Algerine fleet he received his first command, *Epervier*. John was ordered to bring the treaty of peace to Washington, but the vessel was lost at sea in July of 1815. The fourth brother, William Branford Shubrick, served as midshipman and lieutenant on *Constellation* and *Constitution*. In a long naval career he finally reached the rank of rear admiral in 1862. These four brothers, born on a South Carolina barrier island, obviously developed strong connections with the sea, and despite their father's problems with the navy contract fulfilled sucessful naval careers.

Efforts at harvesting live oaks on Bull Island for shipbuilding did not end with Shubrick's failed enterprise. After the War of 1812, a survey of live oaks in the southeast noted that Bull Island could provide timber for three sloops of war. Davis Thacher wrote in his diary in 1817 that Christopher Fitzsimmons, the owner of Bull Island from 1812 to 1833, had bought the island for $12,000 and had gotten $24,000 worth of live oak timber and palmetto logs from it. Various letters from live oakers indicate that timbering efforts were occurring on the island in 1825 and 1841. A letter in 1841 from Mr. Barnabas Hiller, a live oaker for forty years, described living with fifty other men in one house on the island before moving with fourteen other men to another house five miles to the north. The years of live oaking on Bull Island had to have a profound effect on the maritime forest and the population of live oaks. While 40 percent of the live oaks were decimated by Hurricane Hugo, it seems that live oaking had a more substantial devastating impact on these trees. Today, the largest live oaks on the island appear to be located in the grove in front of Dominick House, but even these trees would have been dwarfed by the trees described during the island's live-oaking days. A barrier island covered with trees rivaling the Angel Oak would have been astounding.

I wash my face off at the faucet in the picnic area and walk back to the refuge dock. Tied up on the outside is the boat of a fishing guide named Bentley, and he has brought a vacationing family from Indiana to catch some fish. We talk a little about the tarpon recently caught around the Northeast Point, and the lack of biting insects on the island today. He proceeds to set the hook on a fish and hands the rod off to a young teenage girl. As she pulls the fish out of the water it gives a familiar vocalization, and Bentley introduces her to the sound of a Lowcountry croaker. I say goodbye to this group, and they watch me raise sail and push off into the creek a little before three o'clock. It is partly cloudy but there is still an excellent south-southwest breeze. I am running down Summerhouse Creek and then into Bull Creek with the incoming tide strongly flowing in but barely slowing my run downwind. I head into the bay and think I have held my course long enough to avoid the shoal I ran aground on this morning. But I am wrong. Not only do I have my daggerboard raised but also my rudder has automatically kicked up in the very shallow water. I use my weight to windward to help steer *Kingfisher*, and our passage actually creates some little waves on this shoal from the wake. We are finally clear and now reaching across the bay. *Kingfisher* pops up on a plane and we take this all the way into the mouth of Anderson Creek past an anchored johnboat.

The effortless passage through the creek facilitates a speedy arrival at the Romain Retreat landing. The sail has been so easy that I am perhaps too relaxed and don't realize the lack of water around the dock. I drop the sail into the water and when paddling around the dock I go aground with the daggerboard. Pulling it up I bring black pluff mud onto the deck and do the same with my paddle. Finally, for good measure, the rudder also finds pluff mud. No, this is not pretty, but I'm in and a good washing for *Kingfisher* and me is in order.

1. February sunrise at the Boneyard.

2. *Kingfisher* on Northeast Point.

3. *Kingfisher* and *Island Cat* at Bull Island dock along Summerhouse Creek.

4. Road from dock into the island interior.

5. View of Jacks Creek.

6. Freshwater impoundment in February.

7. Shallow inlet flooding the marsh at high tide between the beach and Jacks Creek dike.

8. View from dunes looking toward Northeast Point and Bulls Bay.

9. Loblolly pine left in the marsh off Turkey Walk Trail by Hurricane Hugo.

10. Bases of well-insulated cabbage palmettos scorched from the reintroduction of fire in the maritime forest.

11. Eastern brown pelicans in Jacks Creek.

12. Duckweed-covered pool at Big Pond.

13. Live oaks are a beautiful addition to the maritime forest on Bull Island.

14. Live oak and Dominick House.

15. Bull Island graveyard where deceased Magwood family members are buried.

16. Tricolored heron in Jacks Creek.

17. Common raccoon in Summerhouse Pond.

18. American alligator sunning in Jacks Creek.

19. Young cottonmouth along the trail to the Dave Clough Wildlife Viewing Platform overlooking the Upper Summerhouse Pond.

20. Aloe yucca, an indigenous plant to Bull Island.

21. Exposed root mass of a loblolly pine at the Boneyard.

22. High tide and high winds at the Boneyard in February.

23. Snowy and great egrets in Jacks Creek.

24. High scarp at road entrance by the Boneyard.

25. Exposed peat section on eastern shoreline.

26. A Lowcountry sunset from Bull Island.

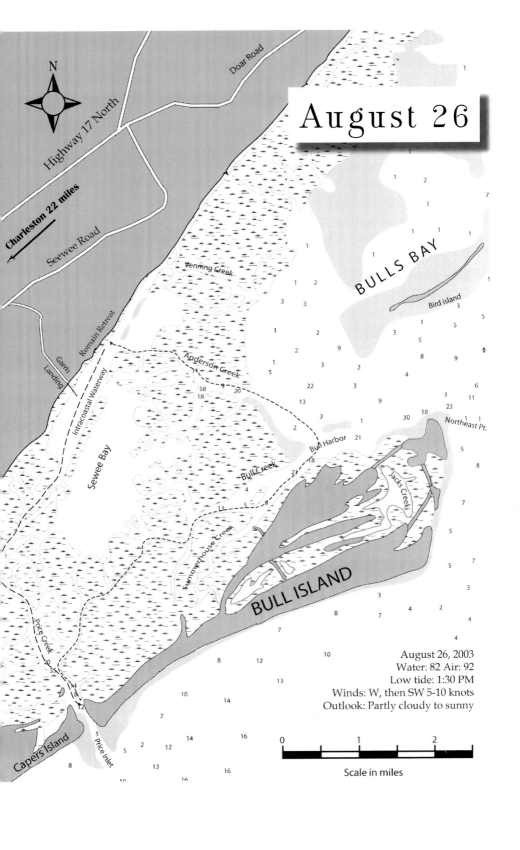

August 26

BULLS BAY

Bird Island

Doar Road

Highway 17 North

Charleston 22 miles

Seewee Road

Wenning Creek

Romain Retreat

Garris Landing

Anderson Creek

Intracoastal Waterway

Sewee Bay

Bull Harbor

Bull Creek

Northeast Pt.

Jacks Creek

Summerhouse Creek

BULL ISLAND

Price Creek

Capers Island

Price Inlet

August 26, 2003
Water: 82 Air: 92
Low tide: 1:30 PM
Winds: W, then SW 5-10 knots
Outlook: Partly cloudy to sunny

0   1   2

Scale in miles

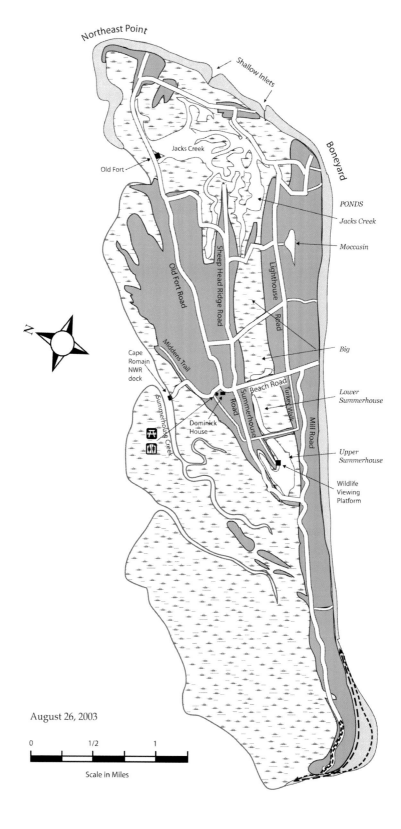

Northeast Point

Shallow Inlets

Boneyard

Jacks Creek

Old Fort

PONDS

Jacks Creek

Moccasin

Sheep Head Ridge Road

Old Fort Road

Lighthouse Road

Big

Middens Trail

Cape
Romain
NWR
dock

Beach Road

Summerhouse
Road

Turkey Walk

Mill Road

*Lower
Summerhouse*

Summerhouse Creek

Dominick
House

*Upper
Summerhouse*

Wildlife
Viewing
Platform

ATLANTIC OCEAN

August 26, 2003

0   1/2   1

Scale in Miles

While making my final preparations for today's sail, I spot about twenty feet off the end of the dock one of our resident landing alligators, measuring about six feet. I cast off and head south down the Intracoastal Waterway with *Kingfisher* closehauled in the west wind. This is quite favorable since I plan to head south to the mouth of the creek to Price Inlet. It is already hot, but the serendipity of this starboard tack allows the sail to shade me from the sun. The sky is quite clear with dots of fair-weather cumulus clouds. The visibility has been great; the nights, the early morning views of the close approach of Mars and the constellations have been spectacular. The beauty of Orion and Mars in the pre-dawn sky appears to be a fine sign for my sail today. Besides seeing *Island Cat* putting into Garris Landing I do not encounter other boats this morning as I did in June, when snowbirds of various descriptions were migrating north. I also do not find greenhead flies joining me as crew, but a disheveled blackbird that alights on my masthead provides a surprise. I have never had this happen before, but the visit is short as my changing sail trim sends the bird on its way. I turn a little to the west as I enter a good long section of the Intracoastal Waterway listed on the chart as Price Creek, and here tacking is required. My daydreaming carries me a bit too far on my tack to the west bank, and I run aground so hard that I am forced to jibe off and come around. I soon make the creek mouth in the eastern marsh and bear off toward the inlet.

I encounter several boats and leave them astern as I run down the creek. The wind has virtually died, but my drifting is greatly enhanced by the outgoing tide. I turn to my chart to note the passing of creek mouths off of this main channel and wonder at the derivation of some of these names such as Santee Pass and Schooner Creek. I notice the quiet of the marsh, soon disturbed by the rustling of several dozen wood storks and great egrets as they take off from a hidden small creek in the marsh. I approach the inlet section of the creek, and on the Capers Island side is Little Bull's Island with a pier, several small buildings and a camper. Power lines cross the inlet here and supply power for Cape Romain NWR needs. Signs of civilization at this end of Bull are a sharp contrast to the Northeast Point. The inlet is peopled with fishermen, picnickers and a moored cabin cruiser. I am seeking a good landing spot to leave *Kingfisher*, and right before the power-line supports I see a steep drop off on the bank. There are some scattered oysters but I find a clear sandy area with a major bonus—a large rusted rod buried in the sand above the high-tide line. This location will serve well as my southern berth on the island.

I grab my gear and head toward the ocean side by walking along the high-tide line and keeping an eye out for the entrance to the Mill Road. As I hike along the inlet the coming of the sea breeze from the southwest is apparent as it fills in the inlet waters and the ocean beyond. The tide is still going out and the thought of the easy sail out the inlet and around the island is tempting. But I have a different plan: I will make a passage from Price Inlet through Bull Narrows, a narrow waterway behind the island feeding into Bull Creek and Bulls Bay beyond. The southwest sea breeze will allow me to sail downwind through these winding waterways. As I walk around the primary beach dunes at the island's end I see a boat right here in the shallows. As I discovered in my June sail around the island, the extensive shoals reach out about a mile, and I can just make out the boat owners at the far point. Across the inlet the shoals also extend out to some distance, and another boat has moored on this shoal quite a distance from the shore.

I decide to continue my hike around this point and down the beach a little, seeking a place for lunch and a dip for relief from the blazing heat. Sighting all the way down to the far point and the beginning of the Boneyard, the curve of the ocean side of the island is pronounced.

I drop everything by a palmetto log and cool off in the ocean. The surf is very tiny and the water quite refreshing. As I eat lunch sitting on a palmetto log, the southwest breeze is blowing fine sand and creating tiny drifts around me. I watch with my reading glasses the sand flecks stirring and building before my eyes. This large expanse of sand on the southern end of the island, with the dunes well set back from the beach, contrasts with the sheared-off point at the Boneyard and beyond. The area between the low primary dunes and the beginning of the maritime forest is wide.

The flooding tide will reach *Kingfisher* soon so I begin my walk back. On the way I take a short excursion out on the large shoal and note that the action of the small waves has created regular ripples in the sand every few inches. The picnickers across the inlet with a shade tent set are still enjoying their day on Capers Island. When I reach *Kingfisher* the inlet waters are lapping under the stern. Before setting sail I am determined to find the entrance to the Mill Road for future reference. Just to the east of the power line and behind a Cape Romain NWR sign is a faint trail through a low dune about twenty-five yards to a sandy turnaround, the southern terminus of the Mill Road. I head up the road and note immediately a sign stating that the road is closed one mile ahead. The road is just a flattened sand area that is quite low, and wetlands bristling with needlerush come right up to it. Cedars are thriving in this sandy area, and old dunes between the road and the beach are being established again with maritime forest.

I turn around shortly and upon arriving at *Kingfisher* realize that she lies at exactly the opposite end of the island from my complementary landing at the Northeast Point snag. It is time to cool off in the inlet and pack up *Kingfisher*. I raise sail, push off into the incoming tide of Price Inlet and run down to the opening of the creek (unnamed on my chart) into the marsh and the passage to Bull Narrows. Quickly I am back in the world of the salt marsh with a labyrinth of creeks and channels, and guessing is definitely not the way to navigate here. After my disaster and humbling experience in Masons Inlet in 1974, the wreck of my boat was only the beginning of a terrible day. That afternoon I also had to deal with getting lost in the maze of creeks behind the island and trying to find my way back to the road where I would be able to retrieve my broken boat. The Laser trailed behind me as I walked through the marsh searching for a passage for most of the afternoon. At times I dragged the boat over marsh, pluff mud and oyster beds. I had missed the passage and struggled physically and emotionally that afternoon to make it back to civilization. I learned a number of lessons that day, and one was the potential for getting lost in the marsh. I now have my reading glasses hung around my neck, my chart sits on deck in front of me and I match up every creek I see with one on the chart.

This labyrinth of hidden waterways and shifting wild inlets of Bull and Price has been an excellent venue for clandestine activities, many of which are not documented but alluded to in various accounts. Located twenty miles north of the bustling seaport of Charleston, the waterways around Bull Island provide some refuge from regulatory officials. In the early days of the colony, rumors surfaced of pirates using the fine anchorage of Bull Harbor that provided access to fresh water at Jacks Creek. Smuggling to avoid tariffs and law enforcement officers has probably taken place here from the seventeenth century up to the present. In 1817 Davis Thacher was invited on board a revenue cutter that was stationed off the island to find slave ships. The last legal slave-trade voyages to South Carolina occurred in 1807, but illegal trading persisted along the coast, and the presence of this revenue cutter suggests that the alarm had been raised for the offloading of slaves here. Unloading of shipments of liquor also occurred here during Prohibition.

The southwest breeze is perfect and *Kingfisher* runs with it. The required changes of course through the winding maze are handled with an occasional jibe rather than tacking. I had concerns about making this run for the first time so close to low tide, but my worries about shallow waters were unfounded. I am engulfed in this marsh world only a little more than one hour after the low tide. My perspective is low because of the cordgrass towering above me on the banks of this steadily narrowing waterway, and the only distant views I have are of the sky above. I am deep in this vast green world of the salt marsh. This green ribbon along the east coast of the United States is most extensive between Albemarle Sound in North Carolina and the northern coast of Florida. Sediments from rivers and streams have built up in the marshes over the years, and the dominant plant residing in the southern marshes is *Spartina alterniflora*. This plant thrives in a saltwater environment that is hostile to land plants due to two conditions: continual contact of the roots with salt water, and immersion of the leaves two times per day in the same salt bath. *Spartina alterniflora* has an elegant system for dealing with the salt water. The base of the plant is about one-half inch in diameter and usually grows from three to six feet tall, but in ideal conditions may reach ten. The root structure is well adapted to anchoring in the soft mud. I recall my first look across the marsh toward Bull Island several days after Hurricane Hugo made landfall in the Lowcountry. A number of Hugo images are etched in my brain, but the view of the marsh that September day in 1989 was quite incredible. Unlike everything on the mainland, with the forest broken, defoliated and brown, there was no evidence of damage or destruction in the vivid green marsh. The salt marsh had nicely weathered the storm since it was deep underneath the huge storm surge that topped out at twenty feet both on Bull Island and on the mainland at Romain Retreat. This tide at Hugo's eastern eye wall has been documented as the highest storm surge on the East Coast in the twentieth century.

The forest of cordgrass provides a rich environment for a number of animals. The marsh grass decomposes into detritus—rich food for animals such as nematode worms, mosquito larvae and that most attention-seeking animal, the fiddler crab. Some fish like mullet also feed directly on the detritus. The colonizing of mud flats by *Spartina alterniflora* also creates protection for wildlife. Some animals come into the marsh-estuarine system only in the summer. Others like oysters, clams and crabs spend their entire lives here. Shrimp are dependent on the shallow rich waters for their maturation. Some of the larger animals, both terrestrial and marine, that access the food supply of the marsh are raccoons, alligators and dolphins. Salt marshes are incredibly productive environments, and no common agriculture practice can produce as much animal food per acre. *Spartina alterniflora* grows continually in the southern marshes. The tide that produces a flow of water over the plants is a major reason for the high production, but the tide also washes about half of the detritus into the nearby creeks and bays, providing food for fish, shrimp and oysters.

A flight of four pelicans cruises low along the edge of the bank, and the tips of the *Spartina* appear to caress the birds' abdomens as they glide and bank to the right to follow the curve of the creek. The incoming tide continues to push me into the waterway that the chart has labeled as Bull Narrows but I recall the 1696 Beresford plat that described the waterway as the "Creek to the other Inlett." I had passed the first main fork earlier to head into the Narrows and now I come to a second fork with the opportunity to head west toward the mainland. I take the starboard fork more toward Bull Island,

and *Kingfisher* is now in the reaches of the much wider Bull Creek and bucking the incoming tide. I keep *Kingfisher* to the south side of the creek to stay out of the main flow and reach toward the island that is now visible to me. Making good progress, I see an island of marsh ahead in the middle of Bull Creek near the intersection with Summerhouse Creek, and I stay to the Bull Island side of this marsh island. There is no activity at the refuge dock, and I set my course close to land to stay out of the main incoming tide in Bull Creek. Bulls Bay is in view and there is an incredible panorama in the clear air: mainland, bay and ocean as far as the eye can see. The poet Robert Woodward Barnwell captured the beauty of the bay in his poem *Bull's Bay*—*"Bowl of Beauty"*:

> *"Old Silver Bowl" was flashing sapphire lights and flame;*
> *And little wavelets crested, white as snow,*
> *As I rowed down the amber tide of Awwendaw,*
> *Hastening to capture joy where briny breezes blow.*

I now run into the spectacularly beautiful bay, sailing freely and prepared to hold this course until I am past the shoal I have continued to mark with my daggerboard. In the distance a white boat is near the Northeast Point and heading in my direction. Taking bearings by eye, I am ready to make the turn for Anderson Creek across the bay to the west and execute the jibe. The white boat off *Kingfisher*'s stern is *Island Cat*, pushing her way into Bull Creek. The ferry is my only company out on the bay besides my usual companions, my scaly and feathered friends. As *Kingfisher* enters the mouth of Anderson Creek my attention is turned to a most familiar bird that I have not seen since the spring migration, a bald eagle. I wonder if it uses the creek as a means of navigation to the island; in the past I wondered if they also used the roof of my house as a navigational aid, often seeing them overhead returning to the mainland around sunset. I now relax in the creek on an easy reach. I am so relaxed that I take a small knockdown during a wind gust. I am taking a drink from a water jug with my foot on the tiller and the sheet wrapped around the daggerboard when the puff hits. The result is a little water in my cockpit and a touch of embarrassment. The sail home is otherwise uneventful with such usual occurrences as the flight of great blue herons and the fining of spot-tailed bass. Arriving at the landing I bring *Kingfisher* head to wind, drop the sail neatly, and steer now with dead stick and an occasional paddle to the inside of the dock.

The landing at Romain Retreat consists of a boat ramp, a floating dock and a fixed pier with a summerhouse. Back in the early 1980s, a small sandy beach to the south side of the pier existed that was adequate for lounging, playing and swimming. Today, *Spartina alterniflora* have completely colonized the little beach and grow under the fixed pier right to the beginning of the boat ramp. I have noted a similar process in Anderson Creek, and imagine that this process is continuing to change the marsh-estuarine world between the mainland and Bull Island.

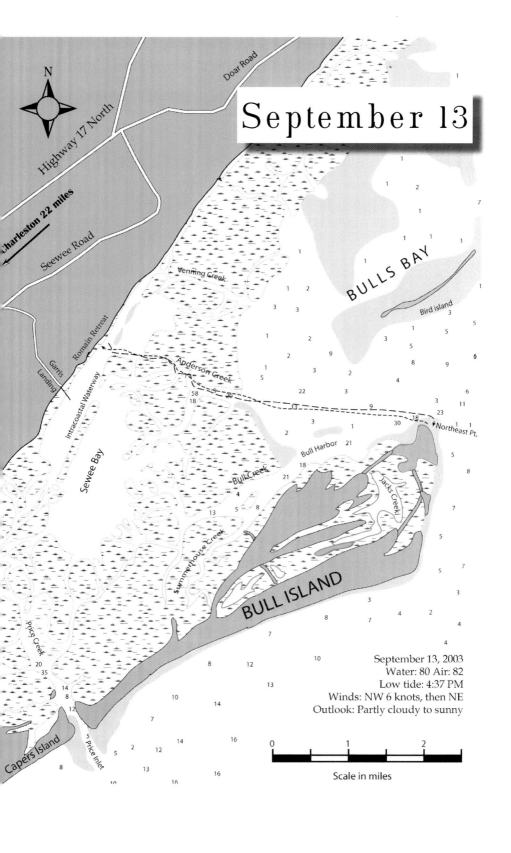

September 13

N

Doar Road

Highway 17 North

Charleston 22 miles

Seewee Road

Venning Creek

Romain Retreat

Garris Landing

Intracoastal Waterway

Anderson Creek

BULLS BAY

Bird island

Sewee Bay

Bull Harbor

Bull Creek

Jacks Creek

Northeast Pt.

Summerhouse Creek

BULL ISLAND

Price Creek

Capers Island

Price Inlet

September 13, 2003
Water: 80 Air: 82
Low tide: 4:37 PM
Winds: NW 6 knots, then NE
Outlook: Partly cloudy to sunny

0   1   2

Scale in miles

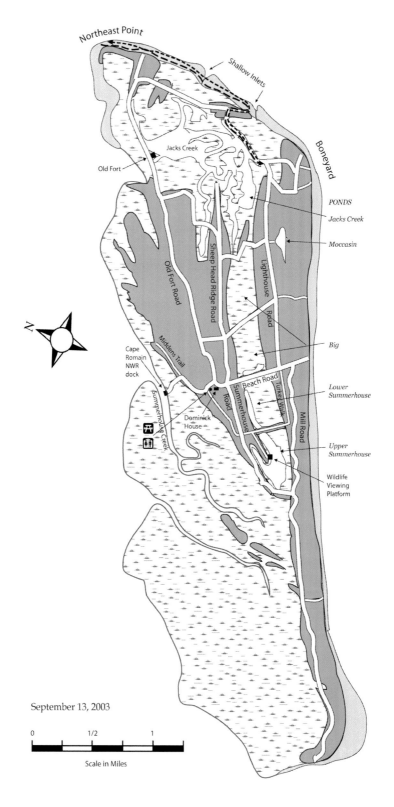

Northeast Point

Shallow Inlets

Jacks Creek

Old Fort

Boneyard

PONDS

Jacks Creek

Moccasin

Old Fort Road

Sheep Head Ridge Road

Lighthouse Road

Big

Middens Trail

Cape
Romain
NWR
dock

Summerhouse Creek

Beach Road

Lower
Summerhouse

Summerhouse Road

Turkey Walk

Dominick
House

Mill Road

Upper
Summerhouse

Wildlife
Viewing
Platform

ATLANTIC OCEAN

September 13, 2003

0   1/2   1

Scale in Miles

September 12 marks the beginning of the shrimp-baiting season, and my neighbors have described early catches as poor. A week ago Hurricane Fabian passed the South Carolina coast, which it left unscathed, on its way to slam Bermuda. A tropical depression has also been hanging around with rains, clouds and unseasonably cool weather along with north winds. Today the sun has reemerged for the first time in a while, but the weather's threat potential is prominent in the awareness of Lowcountry residents due to a true danger, Hurricane Isabel, having reached the unthinkable Category 5 status. Hugo survivors are beginning the preparation rituals; I bought a new flashlight, moved items off my deck and backed-up computer files. With the storm many days off, it is a good day for heading out on the water and to the island. For the first time in my sailing trips this year, I am to have a companion, my neighbor Maurice Snook. Noting my regular trips in *Kingfisher*, he spoke to me about tagging along in his kayak. He has paddled to the Cape Romain NWR dock but never to the Northeast Point. I later analyzed my less-than-enthusiastic response and realized I wondered at his capability. I countered this resistance, wanting to be friendly, and realized there is strength in numbers.

We are to meet at the landing, and the waterway is not showing the six to twelve knots the forecast predicted—it is a millpond. I might be paddling all the way to the island myself. The landing has as many cars and trailers as I've seen there. It is not just the beautiful day, but also the proximity to Bulls Bay, the best shrimp-baiting waters around. I anticipate many boats on the bay and motoring through Anderson Creek. I drop *Kingfisher* into the water and decide to raise sail and mess around while waiting for Maurice. There is a little breeze and I am hoping for more. Maurice arrives, and after dropping in his kayak and loading gear he is off. I notice immediately that he has a fine paddling technique, and he has his kayak chugging across the Intracoastal Waterway. I tack toward the entrance to the creek, and quickly I am trailing in position and speed. Maurice asks if I would like to receive a towline, and I decline his offer. The wind is south-southeast and the more southerly stretches of Anderson Creek require some tacks, but sections of the creek that bend to the east allow *Kingfisher* to reach and match Maurice's kayak speed. It is a banner day in this creek for boat traffic. At the opening to the bay the view is dramatically different from the norm, due to the number of boats. The channel out to the Northeast Point is well marked by boats and the lines of shrimp-baiting poles, mostly white PVC. These lines of poles are the "plots" for each boat. Some people are already working their cast nets, while others are resting or fishing. *Kingfisher* and Maurice's kayak form a procession between the boats on either side of the channel. It is now an effortless reach for *Kingfisher*, and Maurice is working hard with his double paddle to keep up. He probed this area before in his kayak but abandoned the effort due to finding shoal waters, a barrier even for the limited draft of his kayak. Others have struggled with navigating here in the past and accessing the deep channel, but there is no more vivid historic event in these waters than the February 1865 Union invasion.

A Union blockade of Bulls Bay had been ongoing for several years, and the invasion in 1865 was planned to hasten the fall of Charleston by a flanking attack via Bulls Bay and an armed march toward Mount Pleasant. The Confederate defenses included a battery located on the top of the Andersonville Mound overlooking the confluence of the inland waterway and the Andersonville Creek. The invasion using shallow-draft vessels and boats was hindered by bad weather and the lack of a pilot versed with these waterways. The shallow waters of the bay and considerable mud flats were the main barriers for this invasion force. The final landing at Awendaw Creek occurred five days after the assault began. The Union forces struggled to find the channels through the bay and marsh—waterways long known by Native Americans and as familiar to me today as my commute into Charleston.

Our procession across the bay is smooth with just the smallest of chop. As we reach the point, there is one boat tied up there, and unfortunately it is located at my private mooring snag. We go on farther, land and help each other carry our boats up the sandy inlet shore. Help is a luxury I don't usually have. A scan of the waters with binoculars finds shrimp baiters all the way across the bay. Bull Inlet is smooth with little surf, and outside shrimp trawlers pull their nets. It is a peaceful scene despite the shrimp-baiting hubbub in the bay. We have the beach all to ourselves in our walk along the Northeast Point and beyond. There is a blue sky with virtually no clouds, and a light sea breeze blows. We arrive at the first of the shallow inlets to find storm surf has scoured it deeper. Past this inlet Maurice explores sand washover fans back toward the marsh and Jacks Creek dike. I stay to watch shorebirds working the former marsh exposed as peat flats on the beach. Maurice is interested in a bird in the area of one of the overwash fans and with the binoculars confirms that this bird has an injured left wing.

Maurice has never seen this section of the beach before and is impressed with its uniqueness and dynamic nature. Before the next shallow inlet we examine the root structures of the exposed trees sticking out of the sand, details normally hidden below the earth's surface. Somewhat hidden is the entrance to the dike and road system of Jacks Creek, which we now enter. We enjoy the view from the top of the dike looking out on the Atlantic and the beginning of the Boneyard, and inland to the freshwater environment of the impoundment. In the foreground and beyond are the feathered inhabitants of this domain.

After Hurricane Hugo's storm surge broke through the dikes at Jacks Creek, the impoundment reverted to its original status as saltwater estuary, producing quite significant consequences. The disappearance of this large 750-acre body of fresh water had alligators looking for water holes on the island. Without the protection of mud holes below the fresh water, these alligators were exposed to the hard freeze experienced that winter, and it was estimated that sixty to seventy large alligators froze to death along with many smaller ones. While plans were being made to repair the dikes, there was another challenge. Saltwater fishermen were able to access this area by boat via the new inlet, and refuge staff fined two fishermen who entered through this inlet. These fishermen challenged not just the fine but the access to the area, stating it had reverted back to salt water, and took the matter to federal court. Their fines were removed, but they were also told to stay out of Jacks Creek. At least in the newspapers, it became a battle between birds and fish. The Army Corps of Engineers was eventually given the permits by the South Carolina Coastal Council to repair the dikes and restore the freshwater impoundment. Locations in the dikes where the shallow inlets passed through the earthworks were hardened against future battles with the sea.

The shallow inlets are now the sea's memory and will again provide the direction for the water's thrusts in future storms.

Returning to the beach, we stop to snack at the familiar bleached cedar near the second shallow inlet. The beach and exposed peat are changed from my previous visit, another sign of the dynamics constantly at work. The shallow inlet has numerous whelks, and I inspect a couple for inhabitants. The abundance of whelks on Bull Island is striking and an attraction for avid shellers. Cape Romain NWR currently prohibits professional shelling; shellers are limited to one small bag, and the specimens must be dead. While shells now collect on decks and dusty shelves in beach houses, they once served a utilitarian purpose. Archaeologists have studied the creation of tools from whelks at the shell middens of Native Americans. In one study where whelk artifacts were analyzed, these fashioned implements were categorized into groups including adzes, bead and bead blanks, scoops and dippers, hammers, picks and chisels. It seems likely that the shoreline of Bull Island was a whelk quarry for Native Americans.

Farther up the shallow inlet, only eight feet wide at low tide, a school of fish is rocketing through the water. It would be an easy dinner to bag with a cast net. The Waiting Beach past this inlet has its usual assemblage of birds: brown pelicans, black skimmers and other miscellaneous shorebirds. A group of marbled godwits turns as one in the air and settles down with the others. We are all attracted to this spot, and like my feathered friends I find it a fine place to wait. Far beyond the waves, perhaps fifteen hundred miles to the southeast of these peaceful waters, exists the latest phenomenon of nature, Hurricane Isabel, its future dynamics and path unknown.

The tide has turned and so must we, retracing our steps toward the Northeast Point, keeper of our boats. The solitude of the shore is in contrast to the business of the bay. This is Maurice's first visit to this part of the island, and it has been a pleasure to share it with him. I have been here many times, and it is a place warranting many future visits. My knowledge and understanding has grown slowly. The shallow inlets, the peat flats and the exposed tree-root structures all reveal the dynamic nature of the island. The cultural history is also evident in the transformation of salt marsh to freshwater impoundment and later, destruction and restoration. Less visible are the scattered prehistoric antiquities mingling with whelks and cockles along the shore, or the brick fragments that may well be pieces of the nineteenth-century lighthouse. Future revelations wait unearthing.

Our boats are safely sitting high and dry at the point. Maurice has a social function this evening, and we make haste to move our boats to the water and join the incoming tide for the push to the mainland. The predicted wind-shift to northeast is 180 degrees off; the wind is light from the southwest. *Kingfisher* is effortlessly reaching across the bay, leading Maurice's kayak between the growing numbers of shrimp baiters in our return procession. One outboard boater heading our way actually slows to a no-wake speed in sympathetic concern for our relatively frail craft. Maurice is churning the waters behind me to keep up, and I casually find ways to allow *Kingfisher* to sail herself, enabling me to look around and quench my thirst. Occasionally I spill wind from the sail to maintain contact with Maurice. Entering into the mouth of Anderson Creek, the winds are lighter now and Maurice pulls away. *Kingfisher* continues with a slower pace, taking in the serenity of the marsh between the outboard traffic in the creek.

Maurice is following the path of untold numbers of Native American paddlers, utilizing the flooding tide in this deep creek to push back from island to mainland. John Lawson noted the skill of Sewee canoeists and mentioned a Sewee guide who transported his party across a flooded Santee River. He described the Sewees as "excellent Artists in managing these small Canoes." Use of this waterway for commerce with the island was probably as natural as their paddling stroke. Native peoples unnamed would have used this highway terminating at the "town" formerly located at our present landing. The 1919 U. S. Geological Survey map of this area labels this creek "Sewee" and clearly the Sewees were closely associated with this creek and the bay. Lawson himself, after his abortive trip across the bay, possibly crossed here to the mainland, since he described leaving the island and going "thro' the Creeks, which lie between the Bay and the main Land."

Lawson also provided the memorable and disastrous account of an event that greatly accelerated the demise of the Sewees. His recalling of the story told to him by a trader is the only documentation of this incredible tale. Some of the specifics, like the date and the exact place for the launching of this voyage, are absent. It would have had to take place in the later seventeenth century. I imagine the Sewee fleet heading out these waters on an outgoing tide and past the island through Bull Inlet. This of course is speculation, but Lawson's account is both believable and incredible at once. His own words best convey what happened:

The Indians *[referring to Sewees]* . . . *were not content with the common Enemies that lessen and destroy their Country-men, but invented an infallible Strategem to purge their Tribe, and reduce their Multitude into far less Numbers. Their Contrivance was thus, as a Trader amongst them inform'd me.*

They Seeing several Ships coming in, to bring the English *Supplies from Old England, one chief Part of their Cargo being for a Trade with the* Indians, *some of the craftiest of them had observ'd, that the Ships come thence, they believ'd it could not be far thither, esteeming the* English *that were among them, no better than Cheats, and thought, if they could carry the Skins and Furs they got, themselves to* England, *which were inhabited with a better Sort of People than those sent amongst them, that then they should purchase twenty times the Value for every Pelt they sold Abroad, in Consideration of what Rates they sold for at Home. The intended Barter was exceeding well approv'd of, and after a general Consultation of the ablest Heads amongst them, it was* Nemine Contradicente, *agree upon, immediately to make an Addition of their Fleet, by building more Canoes, and those to be of the best Sort, and biggest Size, as fit for their intended Discovery. Some* Indians *were employ'd about making the Canoes, others to hunting, every one to the Post he was most fit for, all Endeavours tending towards an able Fleet and Cargo for* Europe. *The Affair was carry'd on with a great deal of Secrecy and Expedition, so as in a small Time they had gotten a Navy, Loading, Provisions, and hands ready to Sail, leaving only the Old, Impotent, and Minors at Home, 'till their successful Return. The Wind presenting, they set up their Mat-Sails, and were scarce out of sight, when there rose a Tempest, which it's suppos'd carry'd one Part of these* Indian *Merchants, by way of the other World, whilst the others were taken up at Sea by an* English *Ship, and sold for Slaves to the Islands. The Remainder are better satisfy'd with their Imbecilities in such an Undertaking, nothing affronting them more, than to rehearse their Voyage to* England.

One historian estimated that the Sewee population in 1600 numbered eight hundred. In 1715 there were only fifty-seven left. It is sad to consider the loss of this indigenous people who so warmly greeted the colonists on board the *Carolina* just years before this tragedy of the Sewee nation.

Maurice is already gone when *Kingfisher* arrives at the landing. Paddling has become the main power for propulsion to the dock. Returning *Kingfisher* home and putting away some of the gear, I drop on my deck some of the bagged stuff, including a couple of whelks, for cleaning up tomorrow. The next morning I drop the shells into a bucket of water and work on hanging gear up on a line under my deck. I hear a noise above, and it sounds like movement in the bucket. Walking up to take a peek, I see the telltale signs of hermit-crab legs in one of the large whelks big enough for the crustacean to hide away completely in his acquired home. Without hesitation I take the bucket on my bike to a neighbor's dock and walk out to return the animal to its home waters. I encounter a revelation on the long walk out the dock. The crab slowly extends part and then the majority of his body out of the shell, exposing it to my gaze, which the crab seems to return. Is the crustacean showing off, revealing its naked torso, the largest I have ever seen? The purpose becomes apparent: the weight of the torso pitched to the side rights the whelk which allows the crab to position itself below the shell and walk along with the protective shell above. I capsize the shell again and watch the same process repeated. As the crab returns to the marsh with a splash, I reflect on the amends I have just made for taking this creature off the shore. The experience has been a gift—a glimpse into the hermit crab's life dynamic revealed in so dramatic a fashion.

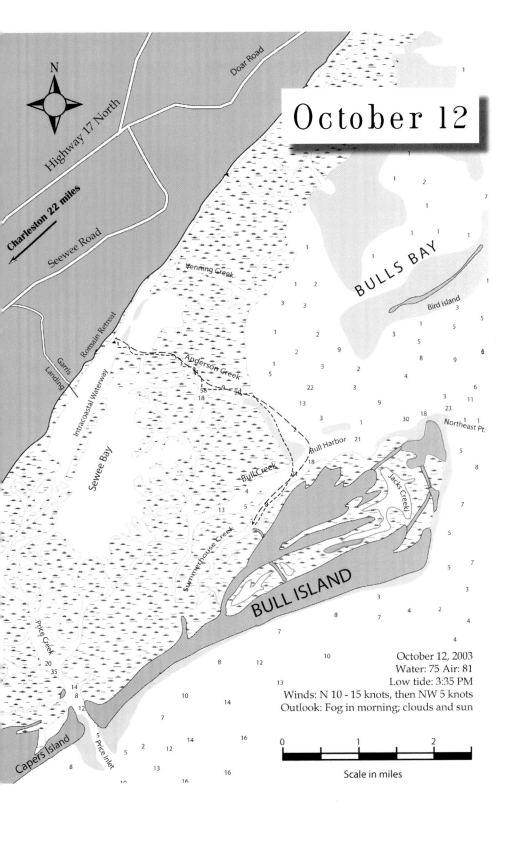

October 12

N

Doar Road

Highway 17 North

Charleston 22 miles →

Seewee Road

Wenning Creek

Romain Retreat

Garris
Landing

Intracoastal Waterway

Anderson Creek

Sewee Bay

Bull Creek

Summerhouse Creek

Price Creek

BULL ISLAND

Capers Island

Price Inlet

BULLS BAY

Bird island

Bull Harbor

Northeast Pt.

Jacks Creek

October 12, 2003
Water: 75 Air: 81
Low tide: 3:35 PM
Winds: N 10 - 15 knots, then NW 5 knots
Outlook: Fog in morning; clouds and sun

0   1   2

Scale in miles

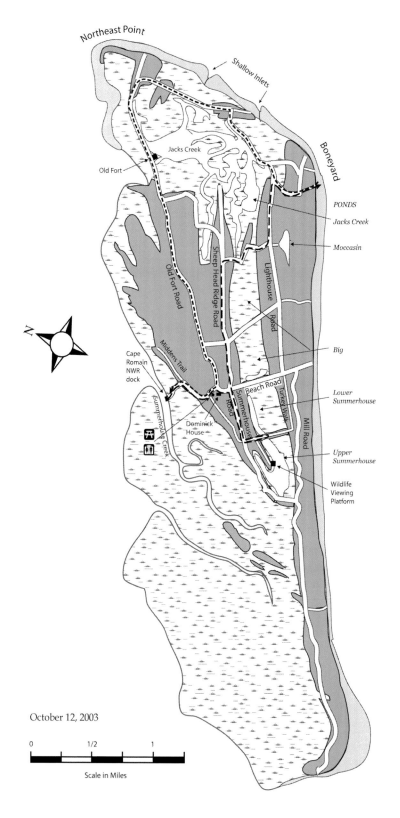

Northeast Point

Shallow Inlets

Boneyard

Jacks Creek

Old Fort

PONDS

Jacks Creek

Moccasin

Old Fort Road

Sheep Head Ridge Road

Lighthouse Road

Big

Middens Trail

Cape Romain NWR dock

Pumphouse Creek

Dominick House

Beach Road

Summerhouse Road

Turkey Walk

Lower Summerhouse

Mill Road

Upper Summerhouse

Wildlife Viewing Platform

N

ATLANTIC OCEAN

October 12, 2003

0   1/2   1

Scale in Miles

When I slide *Kingfisher* into the waterway this morning, Bull Island is not visible through the fog. Scores of gulls add to the atmosphere of the low sky and breeze from the north. I give thanks for this most favorable breeze as I rig, since I have an appointment on the island today. The SEWEE Association is sponsoring a fundraiser, "Day on Bulls Island with Rudy Mancke," and I am registered for the second of the two tours for the day. The ferry *Island Cat* provides transport to the island, but I decide to find my own way on *Kingfisher*. I head out early at 9:20 a.m. to allow plenty of time. The tide is almost slack, and I want to get out to the entrance to Bull Creek before the outgoing tide makes the sail into this creek too unfavorable. After the first main curve in Anderson Creek, a large shaft of sunlight beams down to the earth on the island ahead, and this vertical light corridor moves south on the land before being swallowed up in clouds again. *Kingfisher* cruises over the Shark Hole with dolphins providing the marine animal presence, and the sun pours through, lighting up the whole area. The air is cool but comfortable, and I close reach across the bay in a light chop. I have plenty of company as I see a good dozen shrimp baiters making the rounds, their poles set up to the north of the channel. Others are just getting out and setting their poles in the bottom. I try to stay dry steering through the chop, but spray is on the deck and the sailing is fine. I finally bear off into Bull Creek and am running into the adverse tide that is opposed to the wind from the north. It makes for some steep, small but surfable waves, and I get my bottom wet in the process. I move to the west side of the creek and stay close to the grass to avoid the main tidal flow. *Island Cat* is heading back to Garris Landing to pick up the second tour group. I steer over to the marsh island in the middle of the creek and playing the eastern side, find my boom brushing the *Spartina*. Crossing into Summerhouse Creek I land at the dock just after 10:30.

My early arrival allows me ample time to secure *Kingfisher* to the marsh side of the floating dock. I plan to be on the island over four hours, so I take extra care with various lines and a bumper. I also want to take the opportunity to look for the graveyard I learned exists on the island. Using the directions I recently received after a lecture at the Sewee Center, I begin my search. The first prime area yields nothing, so I head on past a former landing area and bulkheaded section on the marsh. Without luck here I press on to a short road that takes me to the entrance to the nature trail, as well as to another path leading to the main picnic area on the island. I don't remember seeing a graveyard in my walk on this trail earlier in the year, but I double-check anyway and also survey the forest mosquitoes. There is a good crop in the woods and any stop attracts a crowd. I backtrack to look more carefully, including along uncut areas near the marsh, but despite finding some shell middens, I come up graveyardless.

I wander over to the picnic area, and the second wave of passengers on *Island Cat* arrives. Organizers of the tour unpack and set up supplies for the luncheon, and it is far from roughing it—box lunches from the restaurant Just Fresh. I talk to Karen Beshears, executive director of the SEWEE Association and the main organizer of the tours. I ask about the graveyard and learn that my directions were off; it is located on the Summerhouse Road, which we will pass on the tour. It is not long before the other tour group pulls in, and their transport includes a pickup truck towing a trailer with installed seating, and a van. This group follows ours in getting lunch. I talk to a former neighbor and fellow MUSC employee about the first tour and hear some of the highlights, including a peregrine falcon sighting.

I overhear a wife mention to her husband that Rudy Mancke sure looks younger on his TV show than in person. The husband informs his wife that SCETV has been showing *NatureScene* reruns from twenty years ago. It has been quite a run for Rudy and the *NatureScene* shows, which have covered fully the natural history of the state, and in more recent years moved to a national and international level. Bull Island has been featured on several shows and included a before and after look at the island with respect to

Hurricane Hugo. If there were such a thing as State Naturalist Laureate, Rudy would be a shoo-in. The group is gathered together after lunch for a recognition and thank you for Rudy Mancke, who has been doing the tours and fundraisers for eight straight years. Karen Beshears and Larry Davis of CPNWR both offer their thanks and several special awards—bird versions of teddy bears. From the first, Rudy is funny, interested and warm. Our group is given the word to get a place in the vehicles for the tour. The trailer is already filled when I get there, so I hop on the back of the pickup. The last person to get on board is Rudy, who takes the seat right across from me.

It is easy to strike up a conversation with Rudy, and I recall doing a walk with him years ago at Palmetto Islands County Park. I ask him about naturalists from the past who have visited Bull Island, and the first one that comes to his mind is Rachel Carson. Rudy talks about various scholars in the biological sciences that came here to meet, study and take in the impressive natural offerings. While Cape Island has been a magnet for nesting loggerhead turtles and Marsh Island for nesting seabirds, Bull Island has been a powerful draw for naturalists. Rudy is just one in a long line of talented naturalists who have turned their expertise to the natural history of Bull Island. Dominick House once was utilized as lodging for guests and was a veritable bed-and-breakfast for visiting naturalists.

One of the early historic naturalists to visit the island was John Lawson, a young Englishman who, in his travels to North Carolina from Charleston, spent two nights on the island. In his work published in 1709, Lawson gives an early and vivid picture of Bull Island. At the time of his visit, Thomas Cary owned the island, and domestic animals included "a great Number of both Cattel and Hogs upon it; the Cattel being very wild, and the Hogs very lean." Lawson also commented on some less-than-hospitable conditions; "Although it were Winter, yet we found such Swarms of Musketoes, and other troublesome insects, that we got but little Rest that Night." When his canoe voyage was turned back in the crossing of Bulls Bay by a northwest "tart Gale," they returned to Bull Island and spent another night. The Indians in their party were sent to hunt and with little trouble produced deer, wild hogs and raccoons. The party also partook in the bountiful shellfish, and Lawson commented, "We had great Store of oysters, Conks, and Clanns, a large sort of Cockles." Lawson described further the bounty of edible wildlife: "These Parts being very well furnish'd with Shell-fish, Turtle of several Sorts, but few or none of the green, with other Sorts of Salt-water Fish, and in the Season, good Plenty of Fowl, as

Curleus, Gulls, Gannets, and Pelicans, besides Duck and Mallard, Geese, Swans, Teal, Widgeon, etc."

Perhaps John James Audubon and John Bachman also visited; many individuals have come with the awareness to appreciate the natural richness of this island. The famous photographer of birds in the 1940s through the 1960s, Allan D. Cruikshank, described his study and photography of birds at Jacks Creek in 1941. He spent about four eight-hour sessions in a blind there and watched a succession of birds come to the bait of dead fish. A postcard with a photo of Summerhouse Pond by Cruikshank announced the conducting of Audubon Wildlife Tours on the island in the 1940s.

Thinking of other naturalists, Rudy remembers a researcher who did some excellent research on sandpipers, but doesn't recall his name. This is probably the only lapse in his memory for the entire day. One of the things about Rudy that I have always been impressed with is his encyclopedic fund of knowledge, and he explains his practice of keeping notes and ledgers, starting while in junior high school. Rudy continues to chat with our group, noticing things around us as we head up the Beach Road and take the first right on Summerhouse Road. Appearing on the right, the graveyard with its fenced-in yard and a small number of visible gravestones is pointed out to us. Our first stop is at the intersection of the Summerhouse Road and Turkey Walk Trail. We disembark and Rudy is off and running. The first individual to get his attention and scrutiny is a bird grasshopper that is handed to him by a tour participant. This is the first of many living things that he not just identifies but interprets: Maypop. Gulf fritillary. Spotted horsemint. *Ilex vomitoria*. Cocoon of a polythemus moth. Duckweed. Blue curls. Tricolor heron. *Alligator mississippiensis*. Spiny-bodied orb weaver. Pink-spotted hawk moth. The list is extensive and grows and grows. But one of Rudy's gifts as teacher is to truly interpret—to discuss processes, relationships and meanings. He looks at the small details (through his always-ready magnifier) and expands to the big picture. He presents some take-home points that echo from his show. One message is that the predator-prey relationship is one of recycling (fly is transformed to become tree frog, or as I joked at lunch today, brownie becomes Bob). The atoms are the same but realigned to take on new forms. Certain characteristics of Rudy Mancke do not come through as strong on his show as in person; he is very personable, enthusiastic, humorous and humble. Like mosquitoes lighting on a traveler, the group flocks around Rudy for his presentations.

Rudy works this area and the tour participants, and tests our funds of knowledge. My fellow participants are fairly knowledgeable, and there are some birders in our midst. Despite the mosquitoes around us, I hear no whining or complaining from this group. Most are content to listen, ask questions, laugh with the group and explore a little on their own. Rudy definitely gets the group laughing when he recounts his grandmother's disapproval of his ideas concerning male and female sex organs in flowers, and how she would refute his knowledge that "was in the book." Everywhere Rudy is looking, catching a butterfly, picking a flower or gall, and noting birds cruising by. On our way to another stop, Rudy notes the carcass of a marsh rabbit and mentions getting its skull this morning, which now occupies a baggie in his vest. Another participant asks about his wife, and if she ever goes along on his field trips. He mentions that she sometimes does and is very supportive of his activities. I ask if this includes toleration of such habits as putting a marsh rabbit's skull in his vest, and he shares that she has seen much more. Rudy mentions the largest animal he ever brought home, a black bear found dead on the road, which now resides in the state museum.

Our last of three interpretive stops is at the intersection of the Lighthouse Road and a path to the Boneyard. I have used this access to the beach several times this year, but Rudy brings out new features to my awareness. I learn of a new tree right here, a thorny small tree with compound leaves. Someone guesses it is a devil's walking stick, but it looks different and in fact is a toothache tree, or prickly oak. Rudy talks about the problems with common names, and knowing scientific names has served him well in travels around the world. He mentions the common name of one magnolia being "bull bay," which obviously creates confusion with the bay family. But this problem of nomenclature is not isolated to botanical species. The island itself and the surrounding waters have their own name problems. The Sewee name for the island was Onisecaw, which was changed to Bull Island, after Stephen Bull who was on the *Carolina* when she made landfall here in 1670. It is not known how his name became associated with the island since he never had ownership. His name also was transferred to the large shallow body of water north of Bull Island, formerly know as Sewee (reflecting the native people) and now Bull, Bulls or Bull's Bay. Let's not forget on Beresford's map the name "Shee–a–Way Bay" for the label on this body of water. The name Sewee Bay was transferred to a shallow sound between Bull Island and the mainland. Anderson Creek has also been known in the past as Sewee. Many names of waterways have surely disappeared along with the native peoples.

Rudy is now talking about the rearranging of the world through the work of mushrooms, and in the middle of this trail with dense maritime forest and the Atlantic Ocean so close, he asks a familiar question as the energy of some members of our group wanes: "Is this amazing or what?" There is no pretense or rhetoric here—just genuine excitement and the desire to share it. We finally arrive at the Boneyard, and the cameras come out as the bleached remains of trees and root structures become photographic subjects. Rudy discourses on the big picture of barrier islands, but also finds the small again: a moth on a dead palmetto tree, a sea anemone in a pool. I notice that the only person in the group who ignores the edge of the pool and allows his shoes to get wet is Rudy. But from that pool I hear the familiar statement from his show, "Let's head back," and I realize our show is about over.

While at the Boneyard I clearly notice a drop-off in wind, and perhaps there is just a little from the southeast as I wonder about my return sail. Our group loads up with Rudy now in the van. Karen lets us know that we will take the circular route back around Jacks Creek but will not stop unless they see something interesting. I laugh that of course we will see many interesting things but understand our afternoon is getting long. As we continue on this vehicle tour, I talk with several old and new acquaintances in the back of the pickup. One family is from Charlotte, and this couple with their thirteen-year-old son went on a structured birding trip the day before at Huntington Beach State Park. Like myself, their son hoped for Rudy to find and grab a snake, but not today. (During a snake talk earlier with Rudy, I recounted his story of picking an eastern diamondback rattlesnake out of the surf on Edisto Beach, and he told the group further details about this bizarre tale.) Others in the group are locals from Mount Pleasant and McClellanville, and I share mutual friends with some of the new people I meet.

We round the long curve near the Northeast Point and head back up the Old Fort Road cruising by the tabby remains. I know I will be pushed to get out of Bull Creek before the incoming tide gets me, so when we arrive back at the picnic area I say a quick goodbye and take off for the dock while others use the facilities. I get to the dock and hail the captain of *Island Cat*, asking where the wind is. He replies that they will have it directly when they get underway. I shed some clothes and notice the growing irritation of no-see-ums. I quickly stow gear, undock *Kingfisher*, paddle out into the stream and raise sail. I pick up a little southeast breeze, but the island shadows the light wind. Underway and making some progress I find the tide still slack. I have decided to sail out of Bull Creek into the bay rather than go through the more confined ferry route. Off my stern I see *Island Cat* finally with the tour folks heading out, and as they turn for the ferry passage I give them a wave of my floppy hat. My breeze soon dies completely, and I notice both that the bay is glassy ahead and that the tide is beginning to turn. So I rig my tiller extension in the drifting conditions and begin to paddle. I make decent movement in the still water and get into the paddling rhythm. Bait shrimpers are working ahead. I'm sure they are enjoying the smooth water, but I'm hoping to finding some wind or I will have a long paddle home.

I cross over toward the west side of the creek, and as I near the opening to the bay I survey the waters. It is a long paddle around the shoal to get to the channel, and I see no uncovered shoal, only shrimp poles and no wind. I recall during a negative tide seeing a little water closer to the marsh, so I make my decision and cut across this area, pulling my daggerboard all the way out. As I paddle along I begin to find bottom with my paddle, but the depth stays steady. There is no turning back now, and with the decision and rising tide behind me I make good time cutting this corner known to me hereafter as Shortcut Shoal. As I get closer to passing over the shoal and finding deeper water, I see the first life of a predicted breeze but not exactly what I had in mind: a light northwest, meaning I will be beating into it. I take in my tiller extension, reset my daggerboard in its slot and sheet in, beginning the beat toward the mouth of Anderson Creek. I find some variability in the wind and notice my impatience at one point with a desire to pull out the paddle, but I give up on a race to shore and sail as well as able. Some increased consistency in the breeze and the push of the incoming tide finally get *Kingfisher* going a little. I keep an eye out for motorboaters racing in through this creek and give way on my slow beat up the creek. After a long sail I make the Intracoastal Waterway and bring in *Kingfisher* with some extra paddling. As I pull the boat out, the biggest cloud of no-see-ums I have experienced in some time joins me. But unlike John Lawson and his unpleasant night on the island, I have a snug home close by.

November 23

BULLS BAY

Bird island

Venning Creek

Romain Retreat

Garris Landing

Anderson Creek

Intracoastal Waterway

Sewee Bay

Bull Harbor

Bull Creek

Northeast Pt.

Jacks Creek

Summerhouse Creek

BULL ISLAND

Price Creek

Capers Island

Price Inlet

Highway 17 North

Charleston 22 miles

Seewee Road

Doar Road

November 23, 2003
Water: 67 Air: 78
Low tide: 1:08 PM
Winds: SE 5-10 knots
Outlook: Sunny

0   1   2

Scale in miles

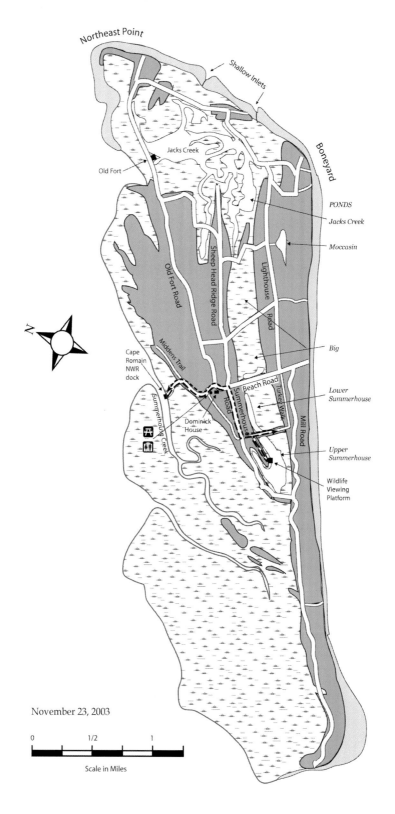

Northeast Point

Shallow Inlets

Boneyard

Jacks Creek

Old Fort

PONDS

Jacks Creek

Moccasin

Old Fort Road

Sheep Head Ridge Road

Lighthouse Road

Big

N

Middens Trail

Cape Romain NWR dock

Beach Road

Turkey Walk

Lower Summerhouse

Summerhouse Creek

Summerhouse Road

Mill Road

Dominick House

Upper Summerhouse

Wildlife Viewing Platform

ATLANTIC OCEAN

November 23, 2003

0   1/2   1

Scale in Miles

It seems like a year since my last sail to Bull Island. I planned to sail two weekends ago, but a flu-like illness capsized these plans. That weekend had strong northeast winds—fun conditions—but the planned sail was not to be. Today, when I bring *Kingfisher* down to the landing and prepare to launch her, I am right back where I was at the end of my last sail: still, glassy conditions and a swarm of no-see-ums hovering around the scene. The air temperature does not feel like November, and I need no more clothing than t-shirt and bathing suit. There is not even a hint of wind when I push off the dock at 10:40, so in a departure from usual practice I do not even raise my sail but instead set up my tiller extension and begin the paddle out Anderson Creek. Low tide will be around one o'clock, so the outgoing flow is pushing me nicely in the smooth creek.

The stillness brings bird sounds out sharply, and I begin to notice the high-pitched sounds of American oystercatchers working the oyster banks at low tide. The shrill noise of the oystercatcher has become as familiar a sound in the marsh as the laugh of the pileated woodpecker is in the woods around my home. The American oystercatcher is a distinctive bird having black-and-white feathers embellished with a large orange bill utilized in opening oysters, mussels and clams. While a common sight around the edge of marshes around Bull Island, it is a threatened species in significant decline. South Carolina is recognized as having the greatest concentration of wintering American oystercatchers in the United States, and a majority of these birds are found around the Cape Romain NWR. However a South Carolina Department of Natural Resources survey in 2001 reported a 21 percent reduction in number of oystercatchers over a fourteen-year period in the Cape Romain area. An aerial survey in the winter of 2002 found three thousand oystercatchers along the South Carolina coast. Seeing these fine shorebirds appears to be a luxury that is threatened.

My progress is not bad with just paddle, and the few little streaks of wind do not tempt me to raise sail yet. I have met only one boat in the creek today, and the end of the shrimp-baiting season has definitely quieted these waters. I detect a filling-in of the wind prior to reaching the Shark Hole, so I promptly raise sail and remove my tiller extension. The wind is ahead of me, so I begin the process of tacking out of the creek. As I head into the bay in the light wind, I hear the sound of dolphin exhalation. They are about a hundred yards out in the bay, but I continue to close with them as their sounds become louder. As I sail by, one of the dolphins catches a little air, perhaps to get a better look at me. The dolphins are soon gone and the wind has done the same. The bay is glassy everywhere. I survey the sail ahead and consider the options: tack around Shortcut Shoal before I reach the deep water of Bull Creek, or paddle across the shoal as I did in October on my return trip from the island. With little hesitation I rig my tiller extension again and begin the paddle across the shoal to take the shortcut.

Before long I am in quite shallow water and pull my daggerboard all the way out. Plumes of mud and surface disturbance indicate fish alerted to my presence. The bay has been so calm that the water is clear in many places, and I am able to see the inhabitants of this shoal. Eelgrass clumps are distributed throughout, and an occasional yellow sea whip appears. I can see tracks across the bottom and assume these are whelks or hermit crabs occupying whelk shells. The bottom is becoming alarmingly shallow, and my rudder begins to drag and kick up. I search for more water without success and finally feel the bottom of *Kingfisher* touch. I get out and begin to drag the boat across until I find a little more water. I realize the tide is still falling, and as I get in and resume paddling I do so with an increased urgency—I don't want *Kingfisher* to be high and dry. I am making good progress both with paddling and pushing off the bottom with my paddle, and I note the depth of the water is between six and eight inches. The top halves of several derelict crab pots are exposed above the surface on this shoal.

I have almost reached the point of the marsh that marks the opening of Bull Creek and deep water. On this final section I see a boat pulled up on the point and a man walking on the bank. I am at most twenty yards off of the marsh bank, and I observe that he is oystering and has about six bushel bags full on the bank. As I am gliding by, he faces me and asks, "Can you help me with something?" I wonder what that could be, and he replies that he forgot to bring water with him, is very thirsty, and could I spare any. I tell him I have plenty, steer toward him and ask him to grab my bow. There is still no wind, and I pull out my thermos as he grabs a water jug. I take a closer look at him, and though he is younger than me, he has both a weathered and haggard appearance. He also is covered from head to boots with pluff mud and has a bleeding knee from a close encounter with an oyster. He is apologetic and thankful as he hands me his gallon jug. It is also covered with pluff mud, and I wonder with him if the inside is also muddy. He is not concerned, and I pour ice water from my thermos into his jug beyond the point where he asks me to stop. He states that his lack of preparation may have something to do with his partying with fellow Clemson fans the previous night after their trouncing of South Carolina, 63-17. I say goodbye and push off, and just a few paddle strokes are needed to make Bull Creek and bear off toward my destination.

The interaction with the thirsty oysterman has blinded me to the arrival of a breeze, which now surprisingly has *Kingfisher* sailing freely down the creek without the need for paddling. It is a light breeze, but I face little opposition from the end of the outgoing tide. I make it into Summerhouse Creek and see at the refuge dock a motorboat and several people. I arrive at 12:30, dropping sail and swinging *Kingfisher* around to the inside of the dock at her usual berth. *Island Cat* also arrives at this time and has only four people on board. I briefly speak to a father and son on the dock. The father is a USC faculty member in marine science and the son a College of Charleston student. They have paddled over here in their red Old Town canoe. This is their second trip to the island, and I give them a copy of a map of the island for their reference. I talk to them some about various parts of the island and walking times for several different places they want to explore toward the north end. We walk a little together down the Beach Road, and we part ways as I turn south on Summerhouse Road.

A primary objective of my trip today is to visit the graveyard on the island and gather information from the gravestones. The graveyard is a short distance down the Summerhouse Road on the right. It is on the edge of the maritime forest, and a good-size live oak tree stands on a back corner. The graveyard has a wooden picket fence in front, and only four stones stand in the enclosure that measures about fifteen by forty-two feet. I pull out my pocket notebook and step into the graveyard, planning to write down the information. I quickly find that this task is easier said than done, since the stones are aged and much of the writing at first glance is not decipherable. So with my reading glasses on I begin to look, squatting in front of each stone. These stones actually appear to me to be made from some type of cement that has been painted and is now peeling excessively. After much study, the first stone finally reveals its information to me:

James Magwood
Born 1838
Died 1905

The second stone has much more information, but is considerably more difficult to read. I squat for a while here, and my perspective changes several times as I observe the natural world at my feet. A tick is climbing up my sock looking for a host, and I notice a trail of ants in front of the stone, their destination a dead wooly green caterpillar. After some time I read part of the stone, though the second two lines do not reveal themselves:

Bessie Viola
———

Magwood
Born 1890
Died 1911

On the third stone, I again fail to read two lines:

Mildred
Magwood
———

Born 1911
Died 1912

The fourth stone is the most difficult, and I realize after some effort that it is also in the direct sun. I decide to return on my way back to the dock and see if have better luck in the changed light.

I walk south on the Summerhouse Road and notice a refuge pickup truck approaching me. The truck stops, and I find that it is Tricia Lynch, a staff member at the Sewee Center. She asks me where I came in on the island and my plan for the day. I realize that one of her responsibilities is to look after the visitors on the island. I mention the people I have seen today and recall talking to her at the Sewee Center. She squints at me for recognition. I notice the antenna on the back of the truck and ask her if she is tracking red wolves. She states that there are no wolves free on the island, and they are trying to get a mate for a wolf in the enclosure. I talk to her about the graveyard and share with her my newly gleaned information. She speculates that Bessie Viola Magwood, who died at age twenty-one, probably died in the childbirth of Mildred. Tricia states that she is looking after visitors on the island and at the same time bird-watching. I reassure her that the southeast breeze and the flooding tide will give me an easy push home this afternoon. We say goodbye and go our separate ways.

I continue along Summerhouse Road until I get to the dike that separates the Upper from the Lower Summerhouse Ponds. This is part of the Turkey Walk Trail that I walked in March. I take a left on the dike and walk a little ways until I get to the trail leading out to the wildlife-viewing platform. This path is on the tip of a ridge, and the peninsula bisects part of the Upper Summerhouse Pond. Palmettos with some live oaks dominate this narrow peninsula. I reach the platform and settle down on the bench for a lunch long-delayed on account of my graveyard research. The plaque on the platform reads:

> *Dave Clough Wildlife Viewing Platform*
> *In memory of Dave Clough*
> *With hope that visitors here share his love of*
> *National Wildlife Refuges and his special joy*
> *in the wonders of natures.*
> *"Come forth into the light of things,*
> *let nature be your teacher." William Wordsworth*

Bull Island provides rich opportunities for nature study and contemplation. Rudy Mancke often encourages people to "slow down and look at the world." Both the casual observer and the dedicated naturalist will find here an environment of wonders and discoveries endowed with ample protection for future generations.

I take the opportunity to watch the birds in the pond, and joining the usual suspects (egrets and herons) is a group of swimming buffleheads. Other waterfowl also cruise by, and I note my limited familiarity with these species. After lunch I make my way back up the trail to the dike, and use this as my platform to look around. An interpretive sign informs me that the Upper Summerhouse Pond covers seventy-two acres and is the most brackish of all the Bull Island ponds. I see the buffleheads take to the air and wheel around both sides of this dike, finally landing in the aquatic growth in the Lower Summerhouse Pond. A sole bird then comes cruising by, and I am cheered to see this kingfisher make his round of this area, land in a tree and announce himself with his familiar rattle. The sound of gentle surf is evident off to the east, and I linger here as I contemplate the route of my return trip.

Due to the time and my desire for one last inspection of the graveyard, I decide to retrace my steps along the dike and back down the Summerhouse Road. This road is sandy, and running across the top of this sand ridge the elevation appears to my eye to be perhaps the highest on the island. The breeze continues to be steady from the southeast and the sky spectacularly blue, beautifully framing the flight of butterflies and birds. A red-bellied woodpecker traverses the air from one tree to another. Ahead a foxtail squirrel crosses and then recrosses the road, exposing his dark color and long tail before disappearing into the maritime forest. Foxtail squirrels and water moccasins were two species with high mortality as a result of Hurricane Hugo. Just ahead is the graveyard, and I take another look at the fourth stone. Without the sunlight, I am able to make out the writing:

Claudette
Wood
Born 1882
Died 1884

I am not sure of the 1882—the "2" is an educated guess. But overall I find the names and dates for the four gravestones and feel some small accomplishment: the feeling of success at learning some new information after some waiting, digging and patience.

So I head for the dock on the familiar Beach Road and the path across the picnic area. Going past Dominick House, I marvel at the beautiful shape of a battered but thriving live oak, a spectacular survivor draped with Spanish moss. I pass no one on the way to the dock and see that the

Old Town canoe is still on the bank. There is breeze in the creek, and I stow my gear, undock and paddle into Summerhouse Creek before raising sail. Immediately I am sailing with ease on a fine reach toward the bay with the bright sun at my back. In these exquisite conditions I see the first sign of clouds low on the horizon in the southwest. The breeze is light but steady, allowing *Kingfisher* to make good progress. I head into the bay, hugging the shoal to avoid the strongest flooding tide. The water is smooth, and I detect a small decrease in the wind as I bear off toward my course to the mouth of Anderson Creek.

There are several outboards scattered around the bay. Before the mouth of the creek the heads of many birds appear moving on our same course, and on closer inspection the numbers increase to several hundred. As *Kingfisher* gains on them, the cormorants skitter off in flight. A dolphin group greets me at the creek mouth. The course is marked all along by floats of crab pots, and the action of one float shows that the speed of the flooding tide is probably doing more work to speed me home than the wind. *Kingfisher* runs freely, and at times to keep the sheet from dragging in the water I push the boom out with the paddle. On the last long straight run of the creek, the lowering sun bathes the marsh grass with a golden hue. With increased clouds in the west I make it to the landing, and see that *Kingfisher* is the last boat to return in the growing dusk.

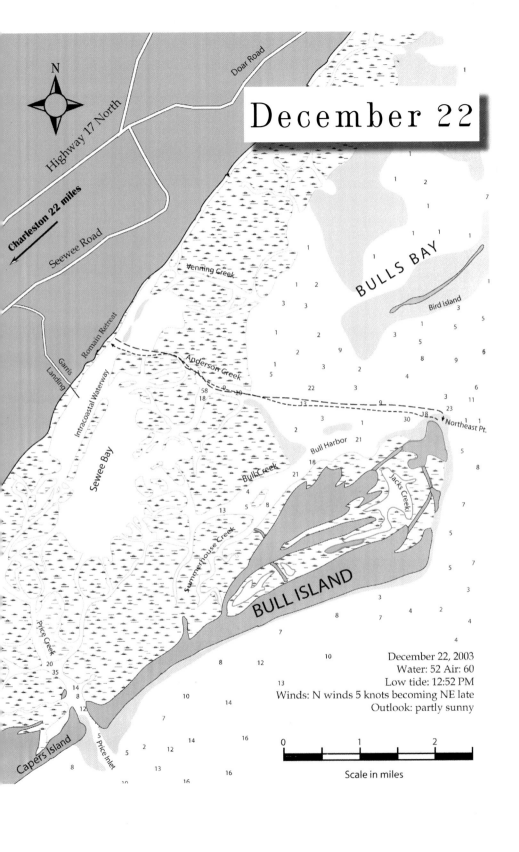

December 22

BULLS BAY

Bird Island

Highway 17 North

Doar Road

Charleston 22 miles

Seewee Road

Venning Creek

Romain Retreat

Garris Landing

Intracoastal Waterway

Anderson Creek

Sewee Bay

Bull Harbor

Bull Creek

Jacks Creek

Summerhouse Creek

BULL ISLAND

Northeast Pt.

Price Creek

Capers Island

Price Inlet

December 22, 2003
Water: 52 Air: 60
Low tide: 12:52 PM
Winds: N winds 5 knots becoming NE late
Outlook: partly sunny

0   1   2

Scale in miles

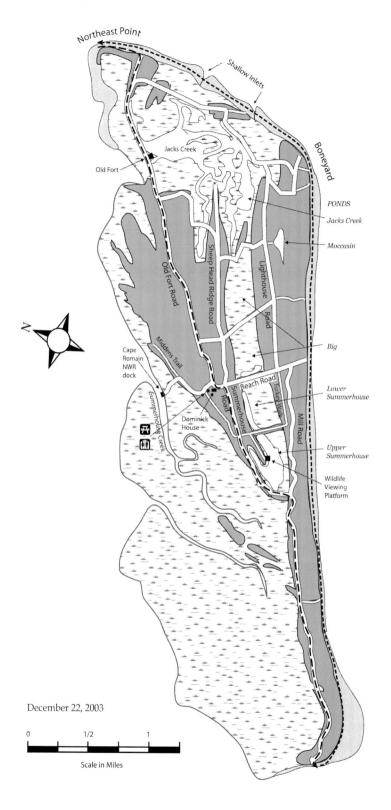

Northeast Point

Shallow Inlets

Boneyard

Jacks Creek

Old Fort

PONDS

Jacks Creek

Moccasin

Old Fort Road

Sheep Head Ridge Road

Lighthouse Road

Big

N

Middens Trail

Cape Romain NWR dock

Beach Road

Lower Summerhouse

Summerhouse Road

Turkel Walk

Summerhouse Creek

Dominick House

Upper Summerhouse

Mill Road

Wildlife Viewing Platform

ATLANTIC OCEAN

December 22, 2003

0   1/2   1

Scale in Miles

I embark early this winter solstice morning, pushing off at 8:20 a.m. in glassy conditions. When I left the house my thermometer read thirty degrees, but this is warmer than the previous morning's low of twenty-two. The sun is up and warming nicely, and I leave my gloves in my vehicle on the bank. I paddle out in the outgoing tide, and the current leaves tiny spinning gyres on the slick surface. The morning on the water is very quiet except for the sounds of construction on the mainland. As I make the second bend in Anderson Creek, I squint into the sun at a bird perched on a crude handmade sign. It flies off and away, and I note the familiar wingbeat of a kingfisher. A great blue heron is scrunched up on a tree remnant in the marsh, and ahead a quintet of oystercatchers comes cruising by. The marsh is alive with bird life this morning: gulls, ducks, pelicans and cormorants. I continue paddling out and recall my friend Rand Schenck, who taught me the technique of paddling a canoe. I think of him, living in Portland and working for Intel, and remember his acknowledgement of the winter solstice. I am brought back to the present moment with a noticeable wave of coolness in the air, much like a current of cold water when swimming. This appears to be the first sign of an impending breeze.

The breeze comes before the Shark Hole this morning, and I successfully raise sail heading downwind and maintaining my course in this light north wind. At nine o'clock I leave the creek for the bay, hearing the shrill cries of oystercatchers. I have the bay to myself except for one boat far out toward Bull Inlet. The visibility is perhaps the best I have ever seen, and I can make out Marsh Island toward the northeast and the line of Cape Romain islands beyond. As I cruise out toward Bull Island with the following breeze, I see that in the boat is a crabber working his pots, and he has many birds in consort. I make the Northeast Point at 9:45 a.m., and I look to find the small outlet to the beach gully that marks the snag I have used for a mooring. I jibe onto the starboard tack and search in vain for this outlet; I am opposing the strong outgoing tide. I see a snag up high, make my landing and am able to step off and keep my feet dry. I pull up *Kingfisher* and survey the scene. I have missed my landing site, and the reason is clear—the beach gully is now a beach pond without an outlet. The snag I see is too far of a reach for my lines, and I walk around the point toward the backside of the island and find a better spot to tie up. The easiest way to move *Kingfisher* against the tide is to walk her in the shallows, so I step into the water and cover the fifty yards paralleling the crabber working about a half mile off the shore. I make *Kingfisher* fast using my mooring line connected to my main sheet. Looking around I notice the crabber is gone, the wind has died and I hear the present background sound of small surf on the shoals of Bull Inlet.

I finish my preparations at 10:15 and begin my walk. I am going to stretch my legs today, and in fact have been planning and anticipating this walk for several months. Although this is the shortest day of the year, my plan is to attempt an inlet-to-inlet-and-back walk. Time permitting, I will take the road and trail system all the way through the interior of the island to Price Inlet, then return via the beach to the Northeast Point. Some time ago I carefully plotted out the predicted tide, so I will return to *Kingfisher* with the incoming tide ready to float the craft and push me home. I am traveling light and have left my binoculars home. I decide to leave my fleece layer on the boat but still carry my hiking stick. There is a fine morning coolness for the walk. I make my way around the point, skirting the closed area of the endangered seabeach amaranth, and step into the forest entrance. Unlike my last walk on this same section in April, there is not a sign of a biting insect, thanks to the previous morning's twenty-two-degree chill. The forest trail has a pleasing cover of fresh undisturbed pine needles. Before long I take the fork to the right and am on the dike of the Old Fort Road. The hedgerows of live oak, palmetto, yaupon holly, bays, wax myrtles and pines leave few views to the Jacks Creek impoundment on the left, but the squawks, beeps and splashes of migratory waterfowl abound. When I peer out through small openings, I trigger the skittering of ducks.

I reach the Old Fort site at 10:45, disturbing the collective of pelicans, cormorants and ducks in the narrow waterway between the water-control structure and the open water of the impoundment. Before continuing on the walk, I step out onto the point and take a look around the impoundment. It is a rich auditory experience with the sounds of the wingbeat of a brown pelican, the squawk of a great blue heron, the skittering of a bufflehead and the distant cacophony of a large group of ducks. Leaving the Jacks Creek sounds behind, I am back in the maritime forest on my walk and spy in the distance a duo of turkeys marching around a bend. I reach a crossroads, noting the left turn where I made my Jacks Creek circuit in April, and then see a quintet of turkeys heading away on the turn to the west. I continue on and pass several other crossroads and paths I have never traveled. All this time I am walking in the opposite direction of the turkey tracks heading my way. I come around a bend just past an area on the side of the road with extensive oyster fragments exposed by plowing, and see the fire-observation tower straight ahead. Making another small turn, the Dominick House lies directly in my sights.

I arrive at the clearing of the picnic area at about 11:30 and push on around to the turnoff for the Summerhouse Road. I stop briefly with my hat off to pay my respects at the graveyard, and carry on past the intersection of the Turkey Walk Trail dike separating the Summerhouse Ponds. The road beyond is soft sand, and I encounter innumerable animal tracks. This path is astride a ridge between the Upper Summerhouse Pond and the salt marsh to the west. I reach the end of this pond, and the dike provides a view both up into the pond and out onto the salt marsh to the south and west, all the way to the mainland. The power line that supplies electricity to the island is strung on poles alongside the dike. Earlier I picked up a feather of some undetermined bird and now decide to grace my hiking stick with it. I wonder how Native Americans here celebrated the winter solstice before the arrival of the Europeans. I read in the past few days of the creation of prayer sticks to mark the shortest day of the year. Collecting oysters for a feast and roasting them on a cold winter day would have been a fine way to celebrate the coming of longer days. Clearly Sewees and earlier native peoples would have had a profound awareness of the travels of the sun in its annual journey, and would have taken note on this distinctive day of the year.

A little before noon I make the crossroads with the Mill Road. An owl drops out of a live oak and flies off. I stop and listen, picking up the sound of light surf to the east. I head south with a renewed pace and detect some sign of light breeze from the ocean. I come upon the junction with the beach path to the left. A sign indicates that the Mill Road ahead is closed between April 1 and September 1; this regulation prevents the disturbance of an active rookery of great egrets, snowy egrets and black-crowned night herons on down the road. The road becomes grassy and a survivor butterfly flies ahead. I am making time now in my push to the south end and note the abundance of palmettos on this very narrow section of the island. There are several low places where the road has been built up, and culverts connect the great salt marsh to the west with fingers of marsh to the east of the road. Sounds of an owl conversation in the distance wafts through an increasing number of cedars. On higher ridges, medium-size live oaks are thriving with the spread of their curved limbs. The forest canopy opens ahead, and a low palmetto is atwitter in the faint breeze. I am startled by a vulture taking flight five yards from the road and see a dead raccoon in the marsh. I come around the next bend and have arrived at Price Inlet at 12:36 p.m.

I am looking directly across at Little Bull's Island on the southwest side of the inlet. I count four roofed structures and two docks, one on the inlet and another on Schooner Creek to the east. On the west point of the island I see the johnboat of someone collecting oysters on this side of the inlet and note a dog standing watch in his craft. I am tempted to walk his way and speak to him, but I am cognizant of the time. I decide to make the return trip via the beach and realize I will need to push on. So I head to the left toward the ocean and find a log to sit on for a short lunch break. I need the rest and fuel. A shrimper is working off the inlet's ebb-tide delta. Past Capers Island in the distance is the unnatural end of the Isle of Palms where high-rises loom. After my short lunch I pause with my eyes closed to give thanks for today and everything I am blessed with. I receive an answer in the exhalation of a dolphin swimming by in the inlet.

I begin the walk back at one o'clock. The beach circuit will be a bit longer, so I know I will not be able to dally. There is a narrow outlet of a gully on the inlet that I cross with a half long jump and half pole vault using my hiking stick. I make my way around this southern point of the island rounding the corner near the dunes. There is a light breeze coming off the ocean, and the coolness contrasts with the brightness of the sun. A second shrimper is working in the distance. The overwash area of the beach that I cut across is covered with shells. The crescent curve of the beach stretches all the way to the Boneyard at the eastern point of the island. Despite the abundance of shells and other flotsam and jetsam, I must temper my inclination for beachcombing. A decomposing pelican carcass lies on the sand. The beach is very wide with the astronomical low tide, and the high-tide line contains more than shells: eel grass, yellow sea whips, starfish, horseshoe crabs, sea urchins and sea cucumbers. I steer off of the high-tide line, descending down the gradually sloping beach, and detect a very fine undulation of ridges of dark sand separated by white sand left in the almost imperceptible sloughs about every foot. At the foot of the beach is a small, long gully before the surf's edge where sandpipers work the shallow water. I do pick up several fine lettered olive shells for Susan, Sara and Eliot.

I come upon the entrance to the Beach Road at 1:40 and see that this is about the middle of the embayment. There is no one in sight, except for the two shrimpers working about two miles off the beach and paralleling my walk. I notice I have assumed a gliding beach pace and wander back to the high-tide line. The surf is a little louder here, but the noise of the shrimpers' engines is also in the background. A vulture on the beach is dining on a large fresh horseshoe crab. I make my way up to the high-tide line again and find an extensive assemblage of yellow sea whips and horseshoe crabs as far as I can see. I add a second feather to my walking stick: this one clearly from a brown pelican. I know I am lagging a bit and can feel my tiredness. I stop for a snack break about two o'clock. The wind has died again, and I realize I may be paddling home. I listen in a tun shell and hear more wind than I can see or feel. Continuing down the beach, the view of the Boneyard now has a mirage-like quality. The frontal dunes are low here, and I see the bounce of a white-tailed deer heading into the sculpted thicket. The pair of shrimpers is now passing me heading southwest. I make my path now by feeling for the firmest sand, seeking the most efficient walking. I pass the first isolated buried trees marking the beginning of the Boneyard ahead. As the maritime forest and the beach intersect at this point, the high-tide line is littered with logs, mostly palmetto. The shrimpers are now dark patches in the blazing area of sun on the sea. The dunes contain numerous ghosts of dead live oaks still standing, while those closest to the scarped dune edge topple onto the beach. I reach the eastern point about three o'clock and pass several familiar paths into the interior of the island.

I leave the skeleton forest of the Boneyard and enter an exposed area of peat. I was mistaken earlier thinking that there were more shells than I had ever seen, for this area is extravagantly littered. The Waiting Beach is quiet today with just a pair of oystercatchers. I reach the first of the two shallow inlets and pull off my shoes and socks, prepared to wade across and go the remainder of the walk barefoot. The southern side of this inlet is sharply scarped, and the height where I prepare to descend is two feet. As I knock my shoes together to remove sand, a section of the scarped sand calves into the water like a glacier. The tide is rolling in, and the cold water feels great on my feet. The long walk has irritated several of my toes, and this immersion is therapy. I pass by the Landing Oak and still note no wind. I find a buried spinning reel and rod and impale it in the high-tide line. As I pass another pelican carcass, I recall seeing over a dozen today. I reach the final shallow inlet at 3:30. I am on the home stretch and calculate that the incoming tide may be reaching *Kingfisher* any minute. I go around the seabeach amaranth area and walk a tangent by the edge of the dunes leading to the Northeast Point. In this flat area I observe an abundant dune plant that I am not familiar with. The leaves have the feel of a succulent. My chosen path takes me across beautifully fine sand, lightly drifting and soft on the feet. Before I reach the beach pool at the point, I notice I am walking opposed to the tracks of my morning prints, and these are flanked by deer tracks on either side. There is a light breeze on the sea oats, and the bay is filled with signs of wind. As I view a section of high dunes at the point, I see *Kingfisher*'s mast standing proud. It is 3:45 p.m., and the incoming tide is just beginning to caress *Kingfisher*'s bottom. What an end to the trip! I am also blessed with a southwest breeze that is perfect for my return sail. Mulling over the completion of my ambitious walk, I still make haste to prepare for the return sail this late in the day.

With all gear stowed, sail up and *Kingfisher* ready to float, the bubble of my perfection is burst with a realization—I do not have my hiking stick. It is not at the mooring snag; I must have left it back up the beach at one of my stops, probably before the final shallow inlet. It is late but I quickly decide to make a fast look for it. I pull *Kingfisher* up about eight yards and with no time to waste run back around the point, barefoot and at a good clip. I decide my turnaround time should be no more than five minutes, both for the lateness of the day and the progression of the incoming tide toward *Kingfisher*. But it is seven minutes when I reach the shallow inlet, and the stick is not sitting on the log there. Perhaps at the next snag—no, it is not there either, and now I must turn around. I definitely do not want to see *Kingfisher* sailing alone across the bay without me. Racing past the beach pond I finally see the sail of *Kingfisher* and slow down to a walk. I have worked up quite a sweat, and the adrenaline surge is slowing down as I contemplate the loss. I must focus on sailing home since it is now 4:25, and I have pushed my return trip later than planned. I turn to positive thoughts, particularly the serendipity of this light but steady southwest breeze that has me reaching across the bay, and the ironic discrepancy with the marine forecast, "becoming NE late." I still have trouble letting go of the hiking stick and consider a return sail later in the week to search for it. But I am reminded of the Native American ritual of making of the prayer stick on the winter solstice. I think back to how I had used bird feathers today to adorn my stick of modern materials— fiberglass, rubber, stainless steel and synthetic line. So the object I left on the shore today is my prayer stick.

I am alone on the bay and can just make out two white craft heading into Five Fathom Creek, miles to the east. They probably are the pair of shrimpers I saw all afternoon. I reach the mouth of Anderson Creek, and after some distance I turn to watch the island and bay receding in the distance. Above the creek heading my direction comes a quintet of brown pelicans following my course, and then banking to the southwest as they take that fork in the creek while I turn to the northwest. The wind is dying, and I supplement the loss of sail power with my paddle. I make the turn to the last long straight section of the creek and hear engine sounds behind me. It is not the sound of a high-speed outboard engine but the puttering of a commercial fishing craft, and when I stand I see a small superstructure above the marsh. I hear her coming, and she finally makes the turn into the creek behind me. I paddle to the marsh edge to leave her the majority of the creek and read the name *Dorothy Elizabeth* as she passes. She is towing a bateau piled with numerous bushels of oysters. We wave to each other and I enjoy her passing as the sole meeting with another craft in the creek today. On one of the last creek bends, there is a close splash directly in front and a surface disturbance of a submarine animal, and then the same disturbance farther off. The wind is gone, but the incoming tide and my paddle are bringing *Kingfisher* home. I see a few small clouds in the west. The sun touches the forest edge on the mainland at 5:11, and the last bit of sun drops down at 5:15. I ghost in to the landing, drop sail and land. It is a beautiful sunset, and those few clouds are now lit up in the sunset glow. Far overhead I hear the rattle of a kingfisher. I haul out my own *Kingfisher* and head home, aglow in my celebration of the solstice.

Several nights after the solstice, I had a dream that I recalled on waking. In this dream, someone returned my lost hiking stick to me. The stick, however, was broken in half.

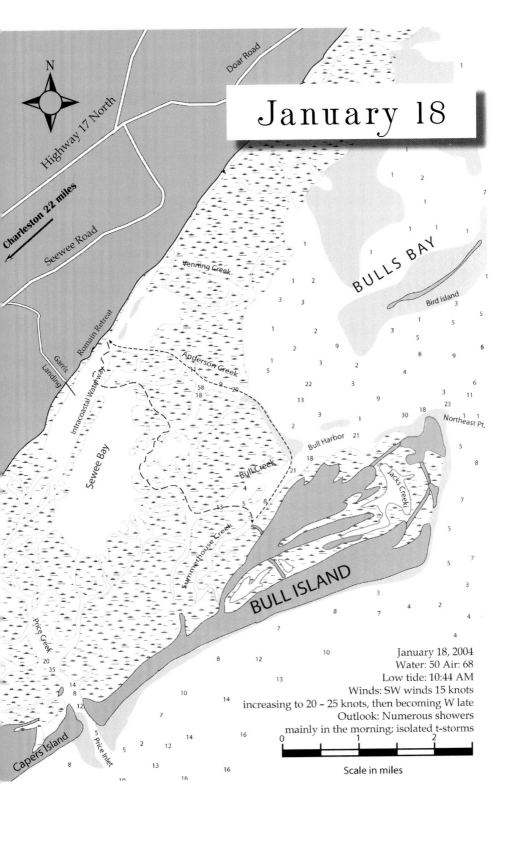

January 18

January 18, 2004
Water: 50 Air: 68
Low tide: 10:44 AM
Winds: SW winds 15 knots
increasing to 20 – 25 knots, then becoming W late
Outlook: Numerous showers
mainly in the morning; isolated t-storms

Scale in miles

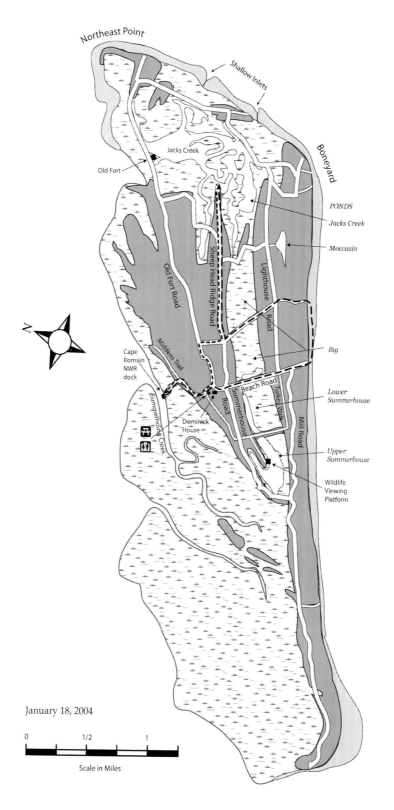

Northeast Point

Shallow Inlets

Boneyard

Jacks Creek

Old Fort

PONDS

Jacks Creek

Moccasin

Old Fort Road

Sheep Head Ridge Road

Lighthouse Road

Big

Middens Trail

Cape Romain NWR dock

Summerhouse Creek

Beach Road

Summerhouse Road

Turkey Walk

Mill Road

Lower Summerhouse

Dominick House

Upper Summerhouse

Wildlife Viewing Platform

ATLANTIC OCEAN

January 18, 2004

0   1/2   1

Scale in Miles

The marine forecast calls for twenty to twenty-five knots of southwest winds later in the day, but when I reach the landing the winds have already reached this velocity. There is a light shower with the wind, and this section of the Intracoastal Waterway exhibits the wave action of a more open body of water. I am reminded that the NOAA marine forecast online also contained in red letters "Small Craft Advisory." *Kingfisher* probably would not even qualify for the "small craft" they had in mind. The conditions today are clearly the strongest winds of my twelve months, and perhaps the biggest challenge. The southwest breeze brings warmer temperatures that should continue to rise today. I suit up with foul-weather pants and jacket as I prepare *Kingfisher* for the journey, and the conditions will demand careful preparations. My rigging includes securing to the boom my new hiking stick—a weathered piece of bamboo scavenged from the marsh this summer. I don't anticipate using this as a tiller attachment unless I have a major breakdown requiring paddling in the absence of sailing ability.

On a visit to the Romain Retreat landing the previous day, I got a good look at a resident kingfisher with my binoculars, and I was surprised when the bird flew down from his perch on a power line and landed on the railing of the dock fifteen feet from me. My view was spectacular: the head, beak and distinct belts of color were viewed in vivid detail. Today, as I get ready to launch *Kingfisher*, I see a pair of kingfishers streak by the dock and curl away to the marsh. I am reminded of two Cherokee legends of how the kingfisher got his bill:

> *Some old men say that the Kingfisher was meant in the beginning to be a water bird, but as he had not been given either web feet or a good bill he could not make a living. The animals held a council over it and decided to make him a bill like a long sharp awl for a fish-gig (fish-spear). So they made him a fish-gig and fastened it on in front of his mouth. He flew to the top of a tree, sailed out and darted down into the water, and came up with a fish on his gig. And he has been the best gigger ever since.*

Some others say it was this way:

> *A Blacksnake found a Yellowhammer's nest in a hollow tree, and after swallowing the young birds, coiled up to sleep in the nest, where the mother bird found him when she came home. She went for help to the Little People, who sent her to the Kingfisher. He came, and after flying back and forth past the hole a few times, made one dart at the snake and pulled him out dead. When they looked they found a hole in the snake's head where the Kingfisher had pierced it with a slender tugaluna fish, which he carried in his bill like a lance. From this the Little People concluded that he would make a first-class gigger if he only had the right spear, so they gave him his long bill as a reward.*

The nature of this one species of bird has been in my consciousness. I have only gained a little insight into the namesake of my sailing craft, with both bird and boat sharing these waters and landing. It seems important to know this animal in deeper ways. Peter Matthiessen, writer and naturalist, discussed in his recent book *End of the Earth* this desire to know other lives beyond humans.

> *To penetrate the consciousness of a wild creature would surely illuminate some vital secret of sentient existence, of pure 'being'. On the other hand, why seek to know? The need for mystery, someone has said, is greater than the need for any answer. Better, perhaps, to be humbly grateful for those last hidden secrets that science has yet to poke into the open.*

The reality of the conditions of my sail is sharply evident after I launch *Kingfisher*, as the wind and waves on the ramp buffet the craft. As I work the boat around pilings on the floating dock, fending off to prevent an early disaster, a barnacle on the piling slices my right hand open from the bottom of my palm down onto my wrist. Blood oozes from the two-inch-long laceration, but after a quick inspection I see that no sutures will be needed. Sailing gloves today will help protect this wound, but it is a small solace for an inauspicious start. I finally am off at about 9:15 and begin my sail to windward, south in the Intracoastal Waterway. My plan is to sail over to the refuge dock on the island via the Bull Island ferry passage. I must first make a number of tacks in the Intracoastal Waterway before I head across the channels through the marsh. The tacking is a battle, and the strong winds are accompanied by more powerful gusts. These conditions provide a very narrow margin for error, and an early tack finds the main sheet wrapped around my head as I struggle to untangle the line before capsizing. I adjust my tacking technique to the conditions by utilizing a more conservative turn than the flat-out roll tacking of racing mode. Several of the violent gusts also include a large directional change, and full-out hiking to balance the craft would, on a backing wind gust, cause the dreaded capsize to windward. I recall a winter sail years ago with my sailing buddy and good friend Alan Held in Wrightsville Beach, North Carolina. We had planned to sail over to Masonboro Island to the south in my Laser, and on this cold day with a north wind we dressed in foul weather gear, rather than wetsuits reserved for cold and heavy weather small-boat sailing. As we left the ramp and bore off downwind, the main sheet was eased too far, and before we knew it we had reached the point of no return and capsized to windward. We both were dumped completely underwater, and we quickly righted the boat and pulled ourselves back on board. Amidst the hurling of expletives we noticed that we were soaked beneath our foul weather gear. We got to the island, but with our drenched clothes and our pitiful bag of homemade muffins soaked with salt water we abandoned our time on the island and headed back home. Such a capsize today would also necessitate a return home, but I could be far from the mainland on this sail.

I tack between the shell-covered bank on the southeastern side of the Intracoastal Waterway, and the mainland and docks of Romain Retreat. One of the docks includes an overhead lift holding a twenty-four-foot Boston Whaler, and contemplating the size of this craft brings to mind the most talked-about fish story in the Charleston area for some time. In the same size Whaler, ten miles offshore, two fishermen encountered what they initially thought were two sunfish swimming about fourteen feet apart. They soon saw that the fins were part of the same animal, and its large size made them think it was a whale. The fish displayed its dorsal fin and white belly, and they realized they were looking at an approximately twenty-three-foot great white shark. The shark swam off for about thirty feet then headed directly for their stern at a rapid clip, stopping inches away from their twin outboards. The head was diamond shaped and about six feet wide. The fish disappeared before they could get a photo. The report by these two experienced fishermen has been viewed as credible, besides being incredible.

Returning to my current adventure, I briefly throw my conservatism to the wind as I squeeze by channel marker number 69. I soon fetch the point marking the opening to the creek of the ferry route and bear off and round into a long straight. My entrance into this straight is accompanied by a blinding breakthrough of the low sun that parts the very overcast sky directly in front of me. The route soon turns into a narrow pass through the marsh, and after several turns my course has me again tacking into the wind. I come to an old familiar place, a channel separated by an oyster bank island creating two narrow channels. I sail past the entrance to allow myself a free sail down to the more southern channel before I tack to begin my effort to get through. Despite my strongest efforts to squeeze *Kingfisher* through on the starboard tack, I can't make it and must tack. I have only a few yards before the marsh bank and work on getting up a head of steam so I will make it through the wind on what I hope is a final tack. Somewhere in the maneuver the main sheet again wraps around my head, and before I remove it I am stalled in irons in this little bottleneck. I must achieve sternway before I can turn *Kingfisher* away from the wind and again move forward on the starboard tack. Somehow as I sheet in I squeeze through the last part of this narrow channel and find a wider channel to continue my course.

I again find myself in a long narrow channel, and the distant end is directly upwind of *Kingfisher*. To compound the adversity, the outgoing tide is flowing against me. I flash back to my February sail almost one year ago, returning from the island in the receding light and wind and at that time tacking against a northeast wind coupled with the adverse tide in this same infernal channel. With little water to sail in, I carefully tack before hitting bottom and make many tacks in this thrash to windward. The strong wind at times stalls *Kingfisher*, and I work hard to not miss a tack again. Somewhere in this battle against the elements, I abandon a possible return sail via an uncharted route. I have been studying both new and old charts and surveys of the area and had noticed a discrepancy between the Joseph Purcell survey of 1793 and recent charts. On this old survey there appeared to be a serpentine passage from Pine Island Creek (now called Back Creek) close to the island and then connecting to another creek, allowing passage to Price Creek and Inlet. But this prospective exploration will not be today—I have more than I can handle.

My current narrow channel borders on a section of Sewee Bay I have never sailed, but I must focus on the last tacks until I finally make the next creek entrance and can ease off to a freer point of sail. I soon am off on a broad reach, and *Kingfisher* accelerates to a full plane. After negotiating several small turns, I bear off again into the full expanse of Bull Creek, and now *Kingfisher* picks up onto an even wilder plane. I am sailing with the full blast of the wind, and besides making sure the craft is in control, I look around for potential sources of breakage. I notice right away a huge strain on the tiller's wood, and I shift weight, adjust sail trim and modify course to ease this strain. Planing for a while, I reach up now on a last section before Summerhouse Creek and cut across a shoal before deeper water, finding bottom with my daggerboard for the first time today. Once in deep water I head up on the last bit of windward work in the southwest blast of wind. I tack up the creek and begin to prepare for landing at the dock. I am surprised to hear two outboards coming from behind me and also heading up Summerhouse Creek, and they are the first boats I have seen on the water today. I realize they will be passing me in this narrow channel, so I quickly tack to leave myself room. They pass me with waves and shared manic expressions appropriate for these conditions. I drop sail a good bit up from the planned landing point, and the wind and tide push me down along the dock until I round up and grab on. It feels good to make this landing, and I pull *Kingfisher* around to the protected inside of the dock and my usual berth, shared today with the carcass of a floating brown pelican.

There is no sign of *Island Cat*, and I am surprised to see Tricia, a Cape Romain NWR staff member, walking up to the dock. We say hello and recall meeting in November on the island. She relates that yesterday twenty-seven people came over on the ferry. She expects that we will probably be the only people on the island today. I walk to the picnic area and drop my gear down on a table while I scribble some notes. I remember my plan to measure the live oaks in the area near Dominick House, but looking through my daypack find I have left my measuring line back on *Kingfisher*. I decide to make the six-minute round-trip run to the dock to retrieve the line. Back at the picnic area I begin a walk around the live oaks for a visual survey. The first prime candidate for impressive size is near the road heading off to the Old Fort and Beach Roads, and I run the line around this tree at the height of 4 feet. After pulling taut, I mark the length on the line with a permanent marking pen. I do the same with two other trees nearer to Dominick House. The measured circumferences, or girths, are 17'8", 13'6" and 15'6", respectively. These are the largest live oaks I have seen on the island, yet they measure less than the largest live oak in Romain Retreat, located near the original homestead of the Andersonville plantation. Former residents, the Reids, called the tree "Boomer," and its girth measures 20'6". This tree, a sibling to the large Bull Island trees cut down by live oakers, was probably not harvested due to its proximity to the Andersonville plantation house.

The house adjacent to this grove of live oaks where I now stand is the only intact historic building on Bull Island. A number of past structures, including the shelters of the Sewees and the live oakers' palmetto-thatched shanties, have easily rotted back into the soil of the maritime forest. The remains of other buildings including the lighthouse, various homesteads of Shubricks, Magwoods, Avingers and Fitzsimmonses, slave quarters and barns remain hidden from view. But the Dominick House survives and now serves as a place for Cape Romain NWR staff to stay when on the island. It was originally built as the winter residence for Gayer Dominick, a Yale-educated New York banker and broker who was also an avid sportsman with a passion for the outdoors. Dominick purchased Bull Island in 1925, and set in motion the development of freshwater ponds to create excellent conditions for a hunting preserve. This required the building of dams and dikes, and one resident of the island, Edward M. Moore, became the superintendent for Mr. Dominick's designs. Dominick had a strong affinity for the island, and as he contemplated his departure from its ownership he realized the risk for such an important natural area. With the development of the Cape Romain NWR to the north, Dominick saw that Bull Island would provide two very important missing elements in the refuge: freshwater ponds for migratory waterfowl and an extensive maritime forest. After Mr. Dominick conveyed Bull Island to the government for inclusion in the Cape Romain NWR, Mr. Moore was employed as the resident custodian. Dominick House was also used as a lodge for visitors to the island for many years, and its register included a long list of naturalists from all over the United States.

After my measuring I begin my walk on the island. I plan to walk on the Beach Road to the shore, and turn north on the beach until I find the first trail heading back into the interior. I will take this across the island on the roads until I get to the Old Fort Road, then look to find the trail connecting to the Middens Trail, which leads back to the landing. As I find myself on the dike crossing between Big and Lower Summerhouse Ponds, the clouds clear off, and I experience bright sun with the continued strong southwest breeze. These are great conditions for drying my wet bottom, shirt, pants and shorts. A particularly strong gust comes through, and several dead palmetto fronds are broken off the top of a tree and blown across the dike close to me. Murphy's Law has surfaced; I decided earlier to carry my foul weather gear on the walk, and it looks as if I will be doing just that—carrying the foul weather pants and jacket, since the weather has definitely cleared. The sound of large surf grows louder as I walk toward the beach. When I reach the intersection with the Mill Road, I look into the dark pond for the belly-flopping gator I saw here last March, but there is no sign of him. I continue my walk through the transition of maritime forest, dunes and beach.

The scene on the shore is like none I have seen in the last twelve months. The strong winds have churned the ocean into a wild vision of surf and breaking waves as far as I can see. Recalling my sail around the island last June, I can't imagine making the voyage in such conditions. Surely the Sewees had seen conditions like these prior to their Atlantic trading disaster and had prepared for this type of weather. The weather that foundered their trading canoes was termed a "tempest," and historically this term was often used to describe a severe thunderstorm. But what had they previously encountered in their paddling and sailing? What was their anticipation of the voyage and what they would experience? What spiritual preparation did they make for the journey? Unfortunately these questions will probably never be answered. The continued strong winds leave a seed of anxiety with me, for I know I will have another round with them on my return trip to the mainland. It is clear that I am alone out here and dependent on both my ability and the soundness of *Kingfisher* to complete a safe passage home. But I return to the present moment, noticing that the sand is scouring the beach clean now, and I am glad my path is taking me downwind. I know that the trail into the interior is not far down the beach, but since it is not marked I walk close to the dunes and search for the opening. I do not stop to pick up any objects on the beach. I am ready for lunch, but will seek shelter in the dunes once I reach the trail. I pass by a sign for the National Marine Debris Monitoring Program, and soon find the entrance through the dunes to this trail after my brisk walk of about twelve minutes from the entrance to the Beach Road.

The path through the dunes provides shelter from the wind and blowing sand but no log for a bench. I sit down in the sand with my lunch but look around and decide to move to a grassy spot. I immediately find that the "grass" is sandspur plants, and I pop up with the intruders impaled on my drying bottom. It takes several minutes to pull about three dozen of these spiked hitchhikers off of my long shirttail. This is payback for the time that my wife Susan sat down on the Jacks Creek dike to look through binoculars at an alligator. She was impaled with several prickly pear cacti, but I convinced her to allow a photograph before removing them. My clothing has protected me from these short spines, nothing like the long thorns of the cacti. I laugh at myself for this little incident and return to my original lunch spot. After completing lunch and taking one last look to the wild ocean scene, I begin the walk into the interior. I come quickly to the low dike through the wetlands on either side of the trail and find on the path a long skeleton of a snake. Despite the fact that its head is missing, it is still as long as my hiking stick. Without the head and with the absence of rattles, I would need Rudy Mancke to identify it. In fact, on previous walks with other amateur naturalists pondering what something was, the usual chorus was, " Where is Rudy?" I shortly come to the intersection with the Lighthouse Road and cross over onto a raised grassy roadway through a low wetland area that a U. S. Geological Survey map identifies as "Big Pond." It is crisscrossed with animal paths. I begin to see a familiar tree in these low areas that has quickly colonized after Hurricane Hugo—the Chinese tallow, or popcorn tree. In one of these groves of twenty-foot-high popcorn trees, I see my first alligator of the day, sunning on a bank of a shallow pool. He is enjoying the sun as much as I am on my walk through Big Pond.

At the intersection with the Sheep Head Ridge Road, I stop to re-secure my foul weather gear from my daypack. I have made a mess of this, and it has been hanging loose and bouncing off the back of my legs. I retie the gear with the line I used for measuring the live oaks, and satisfied that it will not resume a helter-skelter attitude, I pick up my pack and continue on the next leg of the walk. I had noted earlier on this segment of the geological survey map that it is an area of high ground. All along this road on the relatively higher ground is the redeveloping maritime forest. Pines, bays, myrtles, sumacs and live oaks are all in evidence. The tall hulks of debarked and snapped-off large pines are markers of the Hugo violence. My walk appears to be taking me a bit more north than I anticipated, though my bearings are from sighting the sun rather than a compass. But I continue and come to large plantings alongside this road, some appearing to be thirty to forty yards wide. This is a reminder of the agricultural past of the island and the existence of plantations here for many years.

When Joseph Purcell surveyed Bull Island in 1793, 1,357 acres were listed as "planting lands." One crop grown on the island was sea-island cotton, one of the important cash crops of barrier island and sea island plantations. Slave labor was an important component of cotton farming, and slaves were part of the plantation community of Bull Island. One young female slave named Polly Shubrick was owned by Thomas Shubrick and listed as a runaway. When Bull Island was put up for auction in 1847, the description of the buildings on the island included "accommodations for 100 Negroes." The auction also included "a gang of about 50 uncommonly prime NEGROES," and it is likely that these slaves were inhabitants of Bull Island. Stories and legends from the eras of slavery and Reconstruction linger and add to the mysteries of the island's cloaked history: of Old Man Bluebeard with an accompanying banjo player luring unwitting blacks over to Bull Island into servitude; of hangings from live oak limbs near Jacks Creek; and of freed blacks attempting to purchase the island (or a variation—being asked during Reconstruction to settle there).

My walk past these sowings of feed for wildlife continues longer than I anticipated. When I arrive at the next crossroads I realize that I am not where I think I am. How could this be? I am on roads, not trailblazing in the wilderness! A sign marks the return to the shelter, directly back where I have come from. I don't understand and look around at the grassy, curved narrow roads heading off in several directions. I decide to take a side trail that I soon see is marked "Dead End Road." It is a beautiful pine-straw covered path. Unlike the previous road the forest is growing right up to the sides of this narrow road making for a sheltered walk at this time of year, but surely difficult in the bug season. It continues a while but I am determined to find its end. Before long the green and brown of the forest is mixed with a window to the blue of water, and going off the road I walk over to the edge of the forest. I am looking out into a wide expanse of water, but it is an inland body. I continue down the road and spot a blue window on the other side. I find the same thing: a vast inland body of water. It is clear that I am on the peninsula jutting out into the southern side of the Jacks Creek impoundment. I actually contemplated making this walk today, or even a run out to the end and back since it is a path I have not walked. Unconsciously I have been led to it and accept that I must see the end. I drop my pack and continue on. I stop to look at several vistas, and in the brilliant sunlight I see a staggering number of ducks, probably in the thousands. I drop the last of my gear (binoculars and hiking stick), and jog the last bit of the trail. I come to the end of the line and step out to see the entire expanse of Jacks

Creek. This view shows the actual great size and the ringing of the waters by the built, vegetated dikes. Everywhere are great armadas of migratory waterfowl, and I reflect on this expanse of water and the wetlands providing bountiful food for the winged migrants. This unanticipated walk has led me to this fine prominence.

I turn and collect my gear along the way as I retrace my steps. As my mind retraces the path, I understand how I arrived here. When I stopped to retie my foul weather gear at the crossroads with the Sheep Head Ridge Road, I must have turned right onto this road rather than continuing straight across. This understanding is confirmed after I reach the beginning of the dead-end road, for the road crossing here is the loop I had taken back in April when I circled Jacks Creek. Despite my knowledge of the island, I made a wrong turn and am now humbled. Though I could cut over to the Old Fort Road at this intersection, I decide to continue retracing my steps up the Sheep Head Ridge Road to the intersection of my wrong turn. Along the way I notice the stump of a live oak tree on the side of the road, cut off flush with the ground. Tapping my hiking stick on it, I find it hard as a boulder. I reach the intersection of my wayward turn and now take the right turn toward the Old Fort Road. I am rewarded with another reptile, this time live, lying across the road—a three-foot-long rat snake. He also is out to enjoy this very warm January day. Farther on a lone bloom of the state flower, Carolina jessamine, has blown onto the road. The Old Fort Road intersection arrives quickly, and I realize how long of a detour I made this afternoon. The way to the landing is to the left, but I hesitate as I look ahead down another path designated as "Dead End Road." This is where I planned to find the old path marked on the survey map connecting to the Middens Trail. January is the perfect time to head off the beaten path to explore, with an absence of chiggers, ticks and biting insects. But I think of the time and my daughter Sara's planned visit from Clemson tonight, and I decide to stay on the beaten path toward home.

I had walked this section of the Old Fort Road on my long walk on the winter solstice last month, and I note the familiar sights of turkey tracks on the road and the view of the Dominick House on the last section. My experience today has been mingled with humility. The barnacle sliced hand, the butt-full of sandspurs and the wrong turn—all have been humbling experiences. They cannot compare, though, to that most humbling experience in Masons Inlet in North Carolina in 1974 that shattered my Laser and my feelings of invulnerability. While these experiences are all reminders to me of my fallibility and limited knowledge, they are also paths to learning. I ponder these and other thoughts as I complete the walk back to the dock.

That seed of anxiety is still present as I view the water and see no moderation of the wind strength, a condition I would have welcomed. But I do not detect the violent gusts of earlier, and there is not yet a wind shift to the west. There is little decision making needed for my return passage; I will not suffer the ferry passage with the need for windward work. I will run off into Bull Creek and sail across Bulls Bay. This will be the fast way, but without the shelter of the ferry passage until I enter the mouth of Anderson Creek. I make all my preparations, and with the final letting go of my last line from the dock I turn *Kingfisher* to run with the wind.

Off on the port tack I quickly run out of Summerhouse Creek. I negotiate a controlled jibe without carrying anything away and steer out into Bull Creek. The opposed incoming tide pushes up a little tight chop, but *Kingfisher* rides easily over and down the swells. The ride is more controlled than the wild planes earlier today, but I am still making impressive progress. I reach the opening of Bull Creek to the bay in short time, and noting that it is four hours after low tide, I commit to another jibe and set *Kingfisher*'s course on port tack across Shortcut Shoal. From my past experiences I calculate having enough water, and the course on a broad reach has *Kingfisher* on a full plane, effectively reducing the draft as we skim across the top of the shallow water. I am flying on this fully realized plane, and any seeds of anxiety are shed on this perfect point of sail. I catch sight of a speck of white of one other boat far out toward Bull Inlet. Ducks scoot across my course toward the marsh in the distance as water shoots out from the hull of *Kingfisher* and occasionally spurts up from the daggerboard slot. I make it into the opening in the marsh of Anderson Creek and check my watch to see I have made it from the refuge dock in fifteen minutes. Involuntarily in celebration I let out a "YEEEEEE!" drawn from my sailing past—a cry of excitement and joy at the glorious experience that today I share with *Kingfisher* and nature. My reach is no longer screaming but progress is still brisk as I cruise through the familiar passage of the creek and by the Shark Hole without sign of a dorsal fin. I make the numerous bends of the creek and the turn to the west on the long last straight. This course necessitates bringing *Kingfisher* up to closehauled, and I resolve to make the passage on this straight without a tack. So I work the puffs and claw *Kingfisher* off the lee creek side. I succeed and bear off for the last bend and the straight shot across the Intracoastal Waterway to the landing. I make several tacks upwind to prepare for the landing and finally drop sail and steer with dead stick, swinging around the end of the dock and a tied-up boat to a secure spot on the dock. My dock-to-dock return was thirty-five minutes, a record I don't think I will surpass in *Kingfisher*.

I am alone at the landing as I pull *Kingfisher* out and find the same as I tow her into my yard. I take the time at home alone to carefully wash hull, trailer, sail and gear. I raise the sail for drying in the late afternoon light and hang up all the washed gear in a well-rehearsed routine. I note some small cuts in the sail perhaps opening a little more, and the rusted springs of my trailer. I have much gear in the bags I carry to put up, but the process of cleaning, drying and putting away stuff is actually soothing and satisfying. The return of the packed cell phone that I have not used on these trips in the past twelve months, the drying out of my handmade chart, the emptying of the unused extra thermal underwear from my water bag—these are tasks I complete readily despite my fine fatigue as I await the return of my family.

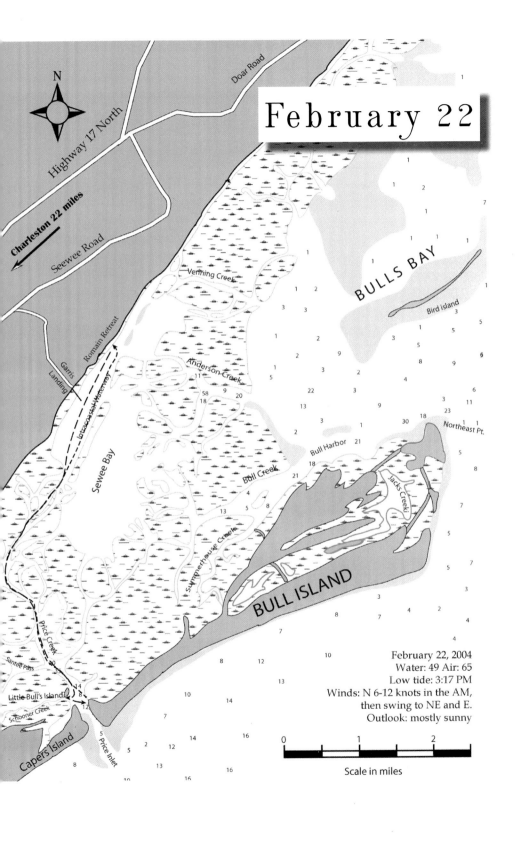

February 22

N

Doar Road

Highway 17 North

Charleston 22 miles

Seewee Road

Romain Retreat

Garris Landing

Venning Creek

Anderson Creek

Intracoastal Waterway

Sewee Bay

BULLS BAY

Bird Island

Bull Harbor

Bull Creek

Summerhouse Creek

Jacks Creek

Northeast Pt.

BULL ISLAND

Price Creek

Santee Pass

Little Bull's Island

Schooner Creek

Capers Island

Price Inlet

February 22, 2004
Water: 49 Air: 65
Low tide: 3:17 PM
Winds: N 6-12 knots in the AM,
then swing to NE and E.
Outlook: mostly sunny

0   1   2

Scale in miles

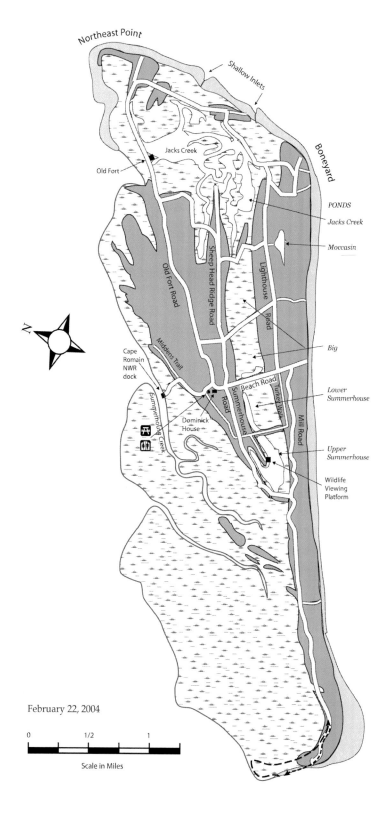

Northeast Point

Shallow Inlets

Boneyard

Jacks Creek

Old Fort

PONDS

Jacks Creek

Moccasin

Old Fort Road

Sheep Head Ridge Road

Lighthouse Road

Middens Trail

Big

Cape Romain NWR dock

Summerhouse Creek

Summerhouse Road

Beach Road

Turkey Walk

Lower Summerhouse

Dominick House

Mill Road

Upper Summerhouse

Wildlife Viewing Platform

N

ATLANTIC OCEAN

February 22, 2004

Scale in Miles

0   1/2   1

This is my birthday week, the time of the year when I first began making the winter sail to Bull Island. Last February marked the beginning of my twelve-month cycle of sailing and walking around the island. My celebration has been delayed with two sailing dates scratched; it has been a bipolar week. I postponed my plan to sail on February 17, my birthday, to allow more recovery time from back spasms starting over the previous weekend. That day the wind was from the northeast at fifteen to twenty knots with rain and a high temperature of forty degrees. Yesterday things were turned around with southwest winds at twenty to twenty-five knots and a high temperature of seventy-five. *Kingfisher* was launched and rigged but encountered rudder problems before casting off. I was not able to make the repair so disappointedly hauled *Kingfisher* home, doing my best to accept this setback. But when I woke up this morning, an idea for repair crystallized in my brain, and after some boring of the rudder mechanism's stainless steel shaft and attaching fittings, I was satisfied with the soundness of *Kingfisher*'s steering system. With mood and wind swinging this week, I am pleased this morning to be preparing to launch. The north wind will speed me toward my destinations to the south. When I do set sail at 11:30 the wind has already shifted to the northeast, and I begin my run down the Intracoastal Waterway.

The wind is brisker than I foresaw, so progress is fast as I cruise past the southern docks of Romain Retreat. One sole fisherman is at the end of Garris Landing pier. *Island Cat* does not run today but yesterday had a full load of passengers returning from the island through Anderson Creek. This alternative to the usual ferry route was required due to the very low tide enhanced by a strong west wind. There is plenty of water in the waterway this morning. A large gull sails by overhead and comes closer to eye me. I imagine the gull's view from above *Kingfisher*. Having turned my awareness to the bird's view, I see an eagle making a return flight to the mainland about one hundred yards off my stern. Farther on brown pelicans stand behind the piled-up shells on the bank with just their heads peering over.

The first boat passes—fine aqua-colored seventeen-foot fisherman with a now-common appendage, an aft poling platform. Its name, *Therapy*, is a reminder of a reason for being on the water. Robert Woodward Barnwell published a series of poems in 1936 inspired by five summers of exploring the South Carolina and Georgia coasts in his bateau, rowing through waterways branching off of the Inland Waterway. In his preface the poet described experiencing a serious bout of depression, and he sought to use these waterborne excursions to "the great peaceful marshes of the coast as a remedy." Many people have looked to the tonic of the coast and its natural wonders, and I count myself in this group of seekers. For me the exploration of natural wonders is immeasurably enhanced by the sailing experience. Experiencing the flow of water past *Kingfisher*'s hull and the wind past her sail are reasons to launch in themselves. *Kingfisher* as a vehicle transforms normal travel to an infinitely more meaningful endeavor.

A small johnboat shoots by heading south and turns into a large opening in the eastern marsh. I follow by bringing *Kingfisher* up to closehauled, and it appears this first section of Price Creek will require a tack or two. But I gradually am lifted off the lee side of the creek and with the aid of the rushing outgoing tide make it by the point into the next section. Now on a close reach I continue to make fine progress sailing through this estuarine environment. The vista ahead looks out to the south end of Bull Island, the power line across the inlet and the hammock of Little Bull's Island on the southwest side. I stay on the north side of the creek and pass the opening to Bull Narrows, noticing the significant amount of current emptying out of this creek. Approaching the south end of Bull Island, Beach Creek opens a last path into the marsh. I learned the name of this creek not from a published chart but from a man very conversant with these waters—Andrew Magwood. Several private mooring buoys are pulled strongly by the outgoing tide and discerning something ahead under the surface, I bear off sharply. It is another mooring buoy submerged by the surging ebb. The johnboat that passed earlier is heading back toward the Intracoastal Waterway. A jibe gets *Kingfisher* headed across the inlet and the strong ebbing current toward Little Bull's Island, my destination.

It was a dark night of cold rain marking the charge of a cold front through the Carolinas when I went to meet Andrew Magwood. I visited Mr. Magwood last month to learn about his family members that had lived on Bull Island and his remembrances of growing up on Little Bull's Island. This island is a small hammock on the Capers Island side, or to the southwest, of Price Inlet. His parents, Clarence Augustus Magwood and Ethel Legare Magwood, raised him and his ten siblings on Little Bull's Island. Mr. Magwood invited me to visit the island, and I now survey possible landings. The pier on Price Inlet currently does not have a floating dock and obstacles include both the distance between the water and the pier and the heavily barnacled pilings. The bank is oyster-covered and similarly not inviting. I recalled in December seeing the dock on Schooner Creek on the southeast side of the island, and I decide to take a look.

I had asked Mr. Magwood about the name of this creek, and he remembered years ago seeing the pieces of the wreck of a schooner in this fairly deep waterway. It separates Little Bull's Island from Capers Island and drains one of the big expanses of marsh. Soon after penetrating this waterway, the creek's superb qualities for landing become apparent with smooth protected water and a triple floating dock just ahead. The outgoing tide is also rushing out of here, and *Kingfisher* runs against the flow as I prepare to land. At once my awareness is filled with the understanding that a number of skilled sailors, fishermen and mariners have made many landings here, and though I am physically alone I must make a decent showing in the opposing forces of wind and tide. I run past the floating docks, round up smartly and drop sail, and steer in to an acceptable landing. The dock is buffered on the creek side with old-fashioned fire hoses for fenders, and *Kingfisher* is royally berthed. I look around at the sights: to my left the south end of Bull Island and Price Inlet, Schooner Creek and marsh straight ahead, and the maritime forest of Capers Island to the south. The power line to Bull Island crosses the marsh heading out to Capers, and as my eye travels this way I see several man-made structures far off in the distance. Refocusing my eyes, I discern these objects as the twin towers of the rapidly progressing new Cooper River Bridge, about fifteen miles off. Returning my focus to the dock and lunch, I stretch out to enjoy the sun and this fine place. Two of the mariners that enter my thoughts are Andrew's father, Clarence, and his brother, Clarence Augustus Junior, known locally to all simply as "Junior." Little Bull's Island already feels very welcoming, and I acknowledge my kinship with the Magwoods. I share the same birthday with Junior, who died in 2001, and his father's birthday falls the day afterward, February 18. Like the elder Clarence, I built my own house and gravitated toward these waterways, marshes and islands years ago.

After lunch I set out to explore this small island, an area of approximately two acres of high ground at high tide. The path from the dock on Schooner Creek appears to be a narrow causeway across the marsh to the natural high ground. The main plants holding things together are cedars, palmettos, yaupons, wax myrtles and marsh cedars. The first structure is a sight, an Airstream trailer with an attached shed roof sporting a woodstove underneath. Continuing on the path, I pass a small yellow house. Just past it is a small man-made pond with oyster shells composing part of the dike material. A small older clearing is ahead, carpeted with grass and numerous objects indicating the original Magwood homestead. Cinder-block steps suggest the former entrance with built-in planters sprouting unopened daffodils—clearly reminders of Ethel Magwood. According to Andrew she was quite spirited, with the expressions "feisty" and "hell-raiser" coming up in the conversation. Her remarkable energy allowed her to outwork any two men. Her personality contrasted with that of her husband, who was easygoing and mild mannered. Ethel was in charge of this household and ruled it as a firm disciplinarian. She raised eleven children, and did so until 1965 without electricity on the island. Andrew recalled the horror of "wash-days," when he and his siblings had to prepare a large pot of hot water for the hand washing, and his mother had exacting standards as to the right water temperature.

Ethel cooked three meals a day throughout the year, even in the heat of the summer, on her woodstove. The woodpile was also a source of work, criticism (on the quality and dryness of the firewood) and punishment (being sent to do extra firewood gathering). Andrew also remembered rowing with siblings on a flood tide to Buck's farm on the mainland. After the harvest the Magwoods were allowed to scour the fields and pick the leftover vegetables. They would fill the boat, and for the next two days Ethel would can this food for their pantry.

Beyond the remnant steps are a number of pilings, a type not seen in modern buildings. They are clearly fashioned from cedar trees, and they evoke respect for the hard labor getting them here—they were probably floated off the beach at Capers. These pilings represent the spirit of Andrew's father, Clarence. He was born in 1886 on Bull Island, son of James Elliott Magwood and Anna Butler Magwood. Andrew never met his grandfather. James was brother to Robert Magwood, who was joint-owner, with his wife Susan and Samuel Pregnall, of the southern half of Bull Island from 1882 to 1906. James' gravestone was the first stone I identified in my visit to the Bull Island graveyard in November. Andrew recalled hearing several things about his grandfather. One distinguishing feature in later years was a constantly bloody lip, most likely a result of the constant exposure to sun. He also liked his liquor and would ride off to the far end of the island on a mule while drinking from a bottle. He would end up passed out somewhere on the island but his mule would always be right next to him when he returned to consciousness. A newspaper account of the Sea Island hurricane of 1893 mentioned a rescue and relief mission by the tug *Sea Gull* led by a Captain Pinckney. The report also gave details of the wreck of a sailboat owned by Robert Magwood, found on the mainland plantation of Phillip Porcher. But a more human drama recounted the story of two women and their children who survived the storm by situating themselves in the rafters of their besieged and flooded home on Capers Island. James Magwood rescued them the next day by constructing a raft of fence rails and driftwood and floating across Price Inlet to their aid.

Andrew's father Clarence was throughout his life an outdoorsman who earned his living from nature. He hunted and trapped for a living for some time, and the pelts he sold were from otter and mink. He shifted his occupation to captaining sailing vessels utilized for hauling vegetables from farm to market. During his boyhood Clarence had worked in the family's oyster business. Workers at the oyster factory, built on pilings in the middle of Bulls Bay, packaged and shipped the raw oysters. Clarence's first wife, Bessie Viola, died as a young woman, and her grave is one of the four I looked at in November.

The tiny speck of high ground, Little Bull's Island, in the vast marsh along Price Inlet was given to Clarence by his uncle Robert. While living on Little Bull's Island, Clarence owned and harvested oyster beds. Andrew has seen the stumps of posts that once were tall lookouts in the marsh for protecting the beds from poachers. For Clarence fishing was a way of life. Andrew described several methods of fishing on the beach: stop-seining and haul-seining. He remembers one bad year of fishing, when right before Christmas his father made one haul amounting to eighteen hundred pounds This large catch was seen as a providential Christmas present. Andrew showed me the haul-seining boat in a picture a friend had painted for him. Clarence also "fished" for diamondback terrapins and constructed pens to place the captured turtles to await shipping to market.

Andrew once rode out a hurricane behind Bull Island with his father in the twenty-eight-foot *Black Boat*, a gas-powered workboat that they used for the weekly visit to town. Besides delivering seafood to town, they would pick up supplies weekly including block ice, their only source of refrigeration for years. For some time the town destination was Adgers Wharf, though later their town stop was Bob Magwood's on the north end of Sullivan's Island. Clarence built a number of rowboats that Bob Magwood rented for handline fishing at Breach Inlet.

The house that once stood on these pilings I now stand in front of was built by Clarence and reflected his character and that of the barrier islands. A number of timbers for the house came from shipwrecks, both parts of vessels and their cargoes. Included in the house's fixtures was one vessel's copper sink. The isolation of this homestead on this high spot in the marsh created both the adversity and the allure of this life. And it was all washed away by Hurricane Hugo, as the hammock was scoured clean of all structures. It was devastating for the Magwood family, and the pain and loss was still evident when I talked with Andrew. He walked the edge of the marsh on the mainland after Hugo, looking for the house and its belongings, and sadly only found one piece of wood from the building. Andrew recalled crying many a day about the loss.

Exploring this former homestead today, I find Andrew's fine new house he built on the inlet side of the homestead. Relics of the Magwood past are everywhere: bird baths, old plantings, recovered valves and old equipment. Past the remnant pilings and a new privy is the fenced garden. Amazingly, the soil has been transported here, an effort begun by Clarence to provide a kitchen garden. Clarence would make trips over to Bull Island and haul topsoil across the inlet. Andrew had told me about this garden, but I still was not prepared to see the bounty. Rows of broccoli, red cabbage and, of course, collards erupt from the loamy soil. Andrew has continued to cultivate this garden soil; the sources of nutrients are bags of leaves carried over by boat and the waste of commercial fishing, such as fish heads and crab parts. I was joined for my tour of the garden by one of the island cats. When I told Andrew I planned to sail over this weekend, he encouraged me to pick a bag of collards, and I now avail myself of his simple and gracious offer. As elsewhere on the island, rain collection by cisterns provides the water supply. Leaving this remnant of the Magwood's agricultural past, I feel inspired to till my kitchen garden at home.

Skirting the garden on the path toward the inlet pier, I notice under a maturing live oak tree and behind some planted oleanders a granite memorial, etched at the bottom with pictures of a duck and marsh, and the following verse:

> *To each is given a little sorrow,*
> *a little happiness, and a little love,*
> *but here on this island, Clarence*
> *& Ethel Magwood found a lifetime*
> *of peace and contentment.*
> *We, their children, dedicate*
> *this memorial to their memories.*

As I walk out to the Magwood's pier on the inlet, the trappings of commercial fishing are everywhere, and the pier is piled high with crab traps. Old boats of varied provenance lie on the bank. Prior to the Magwoods' efforts in shrimping, they were known in the commercial seafood industry for creating the reputation of the fine flavor of Bulls Bay oysters on the Atlantic seaboard. Ethel put her work ethic into the shucking of oysters and marketing raw oysters to Charleston-area families, including those on the Charleston peninsula. Andrew remembers a tram his father built on Little Bull's Island to transfer the oysters from the dock to the house where Ethel would do her shucking. She would shuck for two straight days, and then she would carry the oysters to Charleston. Their first boat with an engine was *Putt Putt*, an obvious affectionate term for the sound produced by the one cylinder Lathrop diesel engine. Price Inlet was a regular anchorage (as it still is) for sport fishermen and yachtsmen. A great enhancement of this anchorage was the clam chowder that Ethel would make and row out to the boaters, who utilized moorings similar to the ones I passed earlier today. Ethel helped the Magwood family scrape out a living with oysters. Projecting ahead to the future, Andrew expressed concern about what he has seen in the marsh in his oyster beds near Little Bull's Island. He stated that he sees the decline in oysters reaching a climax—dead beds everywhere—in just ten years.

It is time to leave the exploration of this tiny place with such a fascinating history of a barrier island family. The story of the Magwoods is filled with a range of human experience: adventure, kinship, tragedy, romance, loss, pride, adversity and contentment. Earl, Andrew's brother, and his mother nearly lost their lives in their inlet drama in 1955. Unfortunately, a real tragedy for the family occurred on Little Bull's Island when Andrew's brother James Elliott Magwood died of a self-inflicted gunshot wound. My interest in learning about the Magwoods is not finished as I leave Little Bull's Island.

After untangling my bamboo hiking stick from the mainsheet, I tack out of the creek in a still fresh breeze and pass the point of the little island. I sail across the inlet with no other boats in sight and land near the angled cable support for the high power pole on Bull Island. I tie up around the rusted stake I had used in an earlier landing and clear some oysters from around *Kingfisher*. I embark on a search for the remains of another former homestead of Clarence Magwood. The Robert Magwood home once stood in the vicinity of the present Dominick House. It was moved off the island on a barge, and part of this house exists today on Magwood Lane in Mount Pleasant. Prior to Gayer Dominick purchasing the island, Clarence had lived in a house on the southern end of the island, a fact I learned from Andrew.

Armed with some directions from Andrew Magwood, I begin the walk along the marsh and across sandy knolls. I am traveling light and wearing footwear for slogging through wet areas. I do not have luck in the first likely spots I explore, so I continue on, following animal trails crossing high spots and flats of glasswort and needlerush. I cut across to the sandy refuge road and decide to walk a little toward the north. Peeking into possible sites, I soon grasp that my search has become the proverbial needle in a haystack. I note that my projected time for beginning the return sail is approaching, but I veer away from my search to explore a high ridge with maritime forest on the ocean side of the road and marked at the summit by a tall antenna used to track wayward red wolves. I walk over the crest, continue down into the maritime forest under a healthy live oak and then transition into pines carpeting the ground with a deep layer of needles. Past the pines is a zone of cedars and thick shrubs, and the growing sound of surf. I retrace my steps and head back south on the road to the inlet. I abandon the search without regrets; despite not finding the old homestead, my explorations have been most fruitful. As with many other voyages in the past year, I have another mission for a future date.

As I walk toward *Kingfisher*, I see a Key West outboard poking into Beach Creek nearby. Getting closer, the sound of the quiet outboard is masked by their radio broadcasting the coverage of a NASCAR race. Before I am rigged and sailing, they are off motoring west up Price Creek. I begin running in the same direction and manage to acquire a wet bottom as I drag my sandaled feet to remove sand and mud. I see the tide is about slack since the lines of crab pots I pass are pointing straight down. The NASCAR Key West boat is puttering into a creek to the north side of the Price Creek, and I sail past. Prior to getting to the entrance to the Intracoastal Waterway, I see a snowbird motoring north. Their wake on the shoal helps me to determine how close I can cut this corner as I round heading north for home. The projected wind shift to the east is serendipitous, since I now do not face a long beat home. I make a gradual turn into a long straight to the northeast. I must now sheet in all the way and work the boat up in puffs and small shifts, hoping to make this section without a tack. After several outboards pass, I have this section all to myself. I become aware of *Kingfisher* slicing through the wind-crafted ripples on the surface. I now am confident that I will make the point ahead without a tack and will round into the more northerly track ahead and a freer point of sail. But over the shell bank ahead I see the upright booms of a trawler and watch him round the point. This longliner has his deck covered with orange buoys. Though I have the point made, I snap onto the port tack, sail right to the edge of the shoal on this side of the Intracoastal Waterway and tack back before the bank. I have given the longliner the channel and kept my options open. The vessel, *Provider*, hailing from Miami Beach, passes without sight of the crew.

I am sailing on a close reach now and ahead see the Garris Landing pier and waterway homes of Romain Retreat. There is more boat traffic as boaters head toward the ramp to pull out. I soon hear a familiar sound, and it is the NASCAR boat bringing me the latest part of the broadcast. I start laughing out loud, and after slowly passing me they finally plane off and move toward the landing. My objection to this is not cultural (I would have similar difficulty with other sports, music or news) but is auditory. The sounds I have heard in the refuge this year—bird sounds, exhalation of dolphins and turtles, wind rushing past my ears and waves lapping on my hull—would have been drowned out by any of this man-made noise. I have had similar experiences in a campground in Great Smoky Mountains National Park and have asked neighboring campers to turn off their Jimmy Hendrix. I enjoy my Hendrix now and then, but that is not what I seek out in the mountains, or out here today. I seek other music on the water, and aspire to tune into other frequencies.

Past Garris Landing and the creek entrance to the ferry route to the island, two fishermen in a Sea Pro are fishing the shoals and having no luck. A bufflehead takes off, flies a circle and comes down with webbed feet waving prior to touchdown. *Kingfisher* joins the incoming waters from Anderson Creek with a push toward our landing. I drop sail and land in very shallow water at the dock with my rudder slicing into the soft mud. It is a very easy landing, and soon the incoming tide allows me to pull *Kingfisher* onto my trailer and up the ramp. Besides the usual tasks I have to take care of when I return home, I make it a point to wash and cook the Magwood collards with dinner.

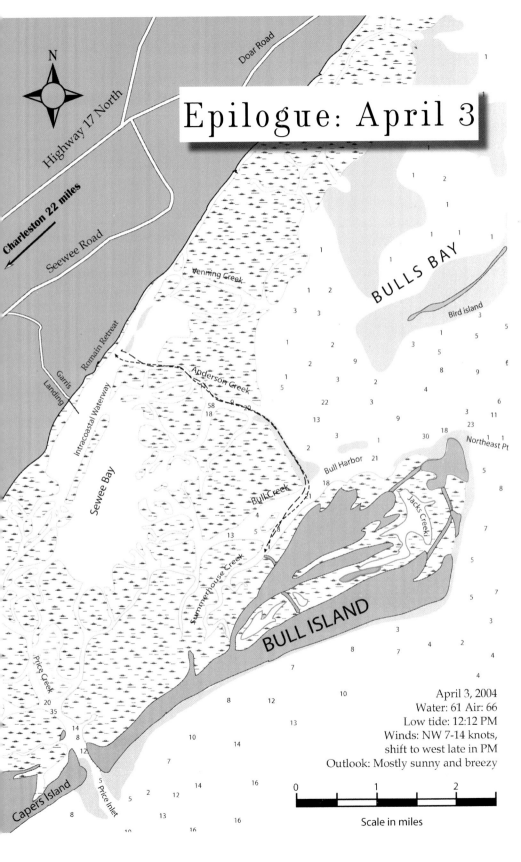

Epilogue: April 3

N

Doar Road

Highway 17 North

Charleston 22 miles

Seewee Road

Garris Landing

Romain Retreat

Intracoastal Waterway

Venning Creek

Anderson Creek

Sewee Bay

Bull Creek

Summerhouse Creek

Price Creek

Capers Island

Price Inlet

BULL ISLAND

Bull Harbor

Jacks Creek

BULLS BAY

Bird island

Northeast Pt

April 3, 2004
Water: 61 Air: 66
Low tide: 12:12 PM
Winds: NW 7-14 knots,
shift to west late in PM
Outlook: Mostly sunny and breezy

0   1   2

Scale in miles

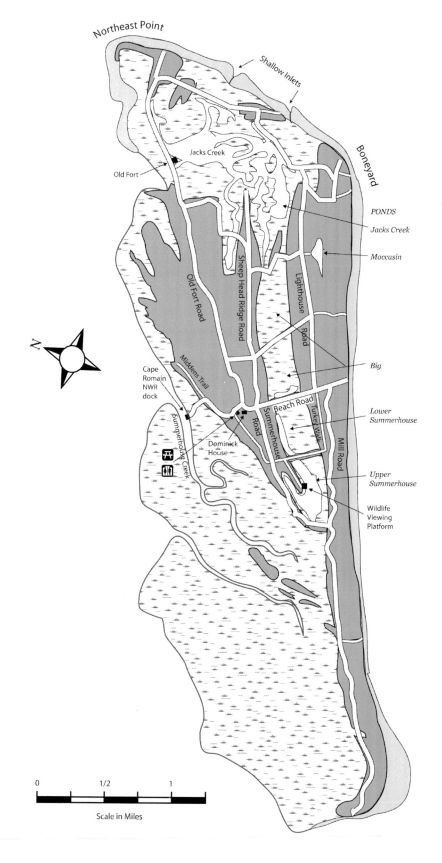

Northeast Point

Shallow Inlets

Boneyard

Jacks Creek

Old Fort

PONDS

Jacks Creek

Moccasin

Old Fort Road

Sheep Head Ridge Road

Lighthouse Road

Big

Middens Trail

Cape Romain NWR dock

Beach Road

Summerhouse Road

Turkey Walk

Mill Road

Lower Summerhouse

Dominick House

Summerhouse Creek

Upper Summerhouse

Wildlife Viewing Platform

N

ATLANTIC OCEAN

0   1/2   1

Scale in Miles

It is the day of the Cooper River Bridge Run, but I am being pulled in a different direction than this annual event I have participated in for the last several years. The experience of monthly sails to Bull Island over the previous year has kept the variables of wind and tide constantly in my awareness, and these conditions are most favorable today. There is an unnamable attraction pulling me to the island through the marsh and creeks and facilitating the bringing of this story to a close. It is in the spirit of this continuing exploration that I cast off *Kingfisher* a little after nine o'clock.

Kingfisher sails easily out Anderson Creek in the northwest breeze, leaving me free to look around. Over the Shark Hole a duet of pelican and vulture circles above. A gull takes the place of the vulture, and finally an ibis joins the pelican as a cormorant beats beneath them close to the water. Even from this position in the marsh near the northern end of Bull Island, the two towers of the new Cooper River Bridge stick out in the distance. Shortcut Shoal is alive this morning with the play of dolphins, and a close-up view reveals scars on the back of one of these mammals. Their activity is not just play but lovemaking, and the intrusion of my presence soon triggers powerful kicks and their disappearance. *Kingfisher* easily rounds into Bull Creek and beyond into Summerhouse Creek, encountering four fishing boats. I quietly bring *Kingfisher* in to her familiar berth.

It is a fine day for a walk on the island, and I choose to head toward the north around Jacks Creek in a loop. The ferry has dropped off a group this morning as evidenced by the coolers left in the picnic area. The well-traveled Beach Road and a turn to the north down Lighthouse Road take me to a short detour, the first trail through the wetlands. There is some recent widening of the trail before the dunes by heavy equipment. Several of the ferry passengers explore the beach. Back on the Lighthouse Road, a strewn-out group of Girl Scouts hurries back toward the refuge dock to meet the noon ferry. They are looking very unprepared for the island experience with many of them wearing flip-flops. Several are soaked up to the waist from their visit to the ocean at the Boneyard. The responsible adults collect the stragglers in the rear, displaying the understandable anxiety of shepherding these pre-adolescent girls. At the intersection of the Lighthouse Road and the trail to the Boneyard, the toothache tree pointed out by Rudy Mancke in October sports new green foliage. A Connecticut couple enjoys the Boneyard after the departure of the Girl Scout contingent and will not leave the island until the four o'clock ferry.

After lunch I continue on the road north onto the dike system around Jacks Creek. My cough spooks a pair of kingfishers that rattle away on the wing. The conditions are perfect for alligators to climb onto the grassy islands in the impoundment to soak up the warmth from the sun. Among the count of about sixteen of these ancient reptiles are some large specimens. I run into my neighbor James Brigham who is fishing with his grandsons on the adjacent beach, and I take them back on the dike to see the largest of the alligators through my binoculars. The excitement of the grandsons' first close encounter (via the binoculars) with these large reptiles is evident.

The sides of the dike are laced with dewberry vines along my solitary path around Jacks Creek. The road continues to grow in familiarity on the way to the site of the Old Fort. Looking at the bit of exposed tabby wall, it seems symbolic of the limits of knowledge appreciated about the island's history. Once past the next crossroads, the signs of controlled burning are starkly evident from blackened earth and tree trunks. I have watched from my vantage point on the mainland the clouds of smoke and the flashes of flame after dark. Perhaps it was my growing feeling of belonging to this place that sparked some concern.

Back at the picnic area at 2:15, ferry passengers are already gathering for the four o'clock return, and one man is lying down and asleep on one of the benches. A friendly and well-prepared (with hats and long sleeves) party of two couples with their children is beginning their walk across the island. I reassure them with the assertion of not finding one mosquito or biting fly on the island all day. *Kingfisher* awaits the return passage as *Island Cat* arrives for the last trip of the day. My expectation of the afternoon wind shift is exceeded by wind from the southwest, past the anticipated west. I see Chris Crolley and Tonya Bernard, the owners of Coastal Expeditions, the company that runs the Bull Island ferry *Island Cat*. They are going to look for their "children," the returning ferry passengers, and I speak to them briefly. In our chat Chris mentions that he saw *Kingfisher* earlier today and recognized that I had a fine wind for the sail over. He now notes that I have a most favorable southwest breeze. He wonders at my karma, and I agree that I am blessed. Chris makes a generous offer of water and other assistance if I ever need it due to breakdown or lack of wind. I thank him and mention the auxiliary power I have used often on *Kingfisher*—paddling.

It is a crowded dock and a solid breeze blows from the southwest, so I cast off and paddle into the middle of the creek before raising sail with some difficulty. I steer sharply to turn *Kingfisher* downwind. With a blast she moves quickly on the run down Summerhouse and Bull Creeks, and I suddenly notice a crack in the top third of the mahogany rudder. The tiller connects to this top section of the rudder, and the rudder to hull connection is on the bottom two thirds, so I face the potential of a major steering problem. Wraps of duct tape from my unused roll would provide temporary support, but I opt for the careful trimming of sail and hull to minimize the rudder needs. The rudder survives several jibes as *Kingfisher* now flies across Shortcut Shoal on a plane. *Kingfisher* makes it into the mouth of Anderson Creek with the rudder crack still noticeably working. Past the Shark Hole a pelican reaches across the wind on our shared course. The final long stretch in the creek brings *Kingfisher* to a close reach requiring more care with the hull trim. A sizable flight of ibis beats by, sharing this same flyway and waterway with *Kingfisher* and heading to the impoundment behind the landing at Romain Retreat. We have the bond of creek, marsh, wind and temporary home.

I prepare for a typical landing in these conditions. The turn into the wind and drop of the sail go smoothly, but the rudder action required to turn *Kingfisher* so the wind is at the stern triggers a solid "crack," signaling the last gasp of the rudder separating from the tiller. I grab the paddle quickly, but before I can turn *Kingfisher* she is about twenty-five yards downwind and downtide of the dock. Paddling halts the backward movement but I make no progress as I paddle hard. I work closer to the marsh of the mainland and consider jumping in to wade and pull *Kingfisher* to the dock. Not ready to surrender to the pluff-mud walk yet, I keep at it with brisk paddling that taps into my energy reserves. The final feet are bridged, and it is satisfying to attach the bowline to a dock cleat.

This final adventure closes another day on the water and on the island. A feeling of satisfaction coexists with the mental problem-solving of the rudder repair in preparation for future launches. It has been a year of study and discovery, and clearly Bull Island and its waters can sustain a lifetime of study. I have learned to appreciate even further my proximity to this special place, and my access to this portal into the natural world. It is a gift to participate in the rhythms of the island's environment, and to observe and follow its endless cycles. The promise of arriving at fresh insights and pondering new mysteries will be a catalyst for an ongoing quest.

Bibliography

A number of primary and secondary sources were identified and used during the research for this book. The reader may wish to explore this information further by referring to the following sources.

Anderson, David G., and Stephen R. Claggett, "Test Excavations at Two Sites in the Cape Romain National Wildlife Refuge, Charleston County, SC." *South Carolina Antiquities* 11, no.1 (1979): 12–74.

Ashe, Dan. "A Century of Conservation." *Endangered Species Bulletin* (U.S. Fish and Wildlife Service) 28, (Jan–Feb 2003): 4.

Audubon, John James. *Audubon and His Journals*. Edited by Maria R. Audubon. Vol.2. Freeport, NY: Book for Libraries Press, 1897.

Baldwin, William P. "The Blockade and Invasion of Bull's Bay." *Carologue* (September–October 1986): 7–10.

———. "James Simmons' Life Ever Lasting." *charleston* (March–April 1991).

———. "Mystery at Saltpond." *Carologue* (Autumn 2000): 22–25.

Ball, Edward. *Slaves in the Family*. New York: Farrar, Straus, and Giroux, 2001.

Barnwell, Robert Woodward, Sr. *Dawn at Daufuskie and Other Poems*. N.p., 1936.

Beston, Henry. *The Outermost House*. New York: Penguin, 1928.

Butcher, Russell D. *America's National Wildlife Refuges: A Complete Guide*. Lanham, MD: Roberts Rinehart Publishers, 2003.

Coker, P.C., III. *Charleston's Maritime Heritage 1670–1865: An Illustrated History*. Charleston: CokerCraft Press, 1987.

Cruikshank, Allan D. "From a Carolina Blind." *Nature Magazine* 34, no. 3 (March 1941): 145–148.

"A Cruise to the Northward," Charleston *News and Courier*, September 1, 1893.

Dalton, Kathleen. *Theodore Roosevelt: A Strenuous Life*. New York: Alfred A. Knopf, 2002.

Dawsey, Sarah. Report on Management Program for Atlantic Loggerhead Sea Turtles in Cape Romain National Wildlife Refuge. 2003.

Dyes, John C. *Nesting Birds of the Coastal Islands: A Naturalist's Year on Galveston Bay*. Austin: University of Texas Press, 1993.

EuDaly, Edwin M. "Seabeach Amaranth Controlled Propagation and Reintroduction Plan." U.S. Fish and Wildlife Service, Charleston Field Office. March 31, 2003.

Fields, John W., Michael P Katuna, and June E. Mirecki. "Relationship of Geologic Framework to Origin of Barrier Island Coast, SC." *Coastal Sediments* 99 (1999): 589–597.

Findlay, Prentiss. "Cape Romain Project Is Under Review." Charleston *News and Courier/ The Evening Post*, May 11, 1991.

———. "Refuge Dike Repairs Need Coastal Council Approval." Charleston *News and Courier/The Evening Post*, June 22, 1991.

Gregorie, Anne King. *Notes on Sewee Indians and Indian Remains*. Charleston: Contributions from the Charleston Museum, no. 5, 1925.

Johnson, Rossiter, ed. *The Twentieth Century Biographical Dictionary of Notable Americans*. Vol. 9. Boston: Biographical Society, 1904.

Kilbey, C.W. "Bulls Island: A Working Partnership with Nature." *Sandlapper* (September 1969): 9–12.

Hay, John. *The Bird of Light*. New York: W.W. Norton, 1991.

Langley, Lynne. "Hugo Damage an Ongoing Problem for Refuge." Charleston *News and Courier/The Evening Post*, July 8, 1990.

Lawson, John. *A New Voyage to Carolina*. Chapel Hill: University of North Carolina Press, 1967.

Leland, Isabella. "Mrs. Magwood Solves Problems of Raising Big Family on Tiny Isle." Charleston *News and Courier*, July 1, 1956.

Leland, Jack. "The Baron of Little Bull's." *The Evening Post*, November 26, 1968.

———. "Bull's Island Weathers Years to Become Wooded Haven." Charleston *News and Courier*, December 23, 1985.

———. "Tiny Island Is a Home to this Family." Charleston *News and Courier*, November 27, 1955.

Leland, John. *Porcher's Creek: Lives Between the Tides*. Columbia: University of South Carolina Press, 2002.

Lennon, Gered, William J. Neal, David M. Bush, Orrin H. Pilkey, Matthew Stutz, and Jane Bullock. *Living with the South Carolina Coast*. Durham: Duke University Press, 1996.

Lofton, John M., Jr. "U.S. Builds Dams on Two Coastal Islands for Fresh Water Ducks." Charleston *News and Courier*, May 15, 1938.

Manning, Phillip. *Palmetto Journal: Walks in the Natural Areas of South Carolina*. Winston-Salem: John F. Blair, 1995.

Matthiessen, Peter. *End of the Earth: Voyages to Antarctica*. Washington, DC: National Geographic Society, 2003.

———. *Wildlife in America*. New York: Viking Press, 1959.

Mongibeaux, Jean-Francois. *Winged Migration*. San Francisco: Chronicle, 2003.

Mooney, James. *Myths of the Cherokees*. Asheville: Historical Images, 1992.

The National Cyclopaedia of American Biography. Vol. 50. New York: James T. White & Co., 1968.

Notice of sale of "Bull's Island and 50 prime Negroes." *Charleston Courier*, February 1, 1847.

Notice of sale of "That valuable island called Bull's Island." *Charleston Courier*, September 15, 1810.

Chestnutt, David R., and C. James Taylor, eds. *The Papers of Henry Laurens*. Vol. 11. Columbia, SC: University of South Carolina Press for South Carolina Historical Society, 1988.

Peterson, Roger Tory. *A Field Guide to the Birds, of Eastern and Central North America*. Boston: Houghton Mifflin Company, 1980.

Pilkey, Orrin H., and Mary Edna Fraser. *A Celebration of the World's Barrier Islands*. New York: Columbia University Press, 2003.

Poplin, Eric C., Christopher T Espenshade, and David C. Jones. *Archaeological Investigations at the Buck Hall Site (38CH644)*. Prepared for USDA–Forest Service, 1993.

Rawley, James A. *The Transatlantic Slave Trade: a History*. New York: Norton, 1981.

Russo, Michael, and Gregory Heide. *Mapping the Sewee Shell Ring*. Prepared for Francis Marion and Sumter National Forests, 2003.

[Salley, Alexander S.] History of Bulls Island. Unpublished document prepared for Gayer G. Dominick.

Sargent, William. *Crab Wars: A Tale of Horseshoe Crabs, Bioterrorism, and Human Health*. Hanover and London: University Press of New England, 2002.

Sexton, Walter J. "The Post-Storm Hurricane Hugo Recovery of the Undeveloped Beaches Along the South Carolina Coast, 'Capers to the Santee Delta.'" *Journal of Coastal Research* 11, no. 4 (1995): 1020–1025.

Slocum, Joshua. *Sailing Alone Around the World and Voyage of the Liberdade*. Norwich, GB: Adlard Coles Limited, 1948.

South Carolina Historical Society. *The Shaftesbury Papers*. Charleston: Tempus Publishing, 2000.

Sprunt, Alexander, Jr. "Treasure Island . . . Both Century." Representative, National Audubon Society.

Sprunt, Alexander, Jr., and E.B. Chamberlain. *South Carolina Bird Life*. Rev. ed. Columbia: University of South Carolina Press, 1970.

Teal, John, and Mildred Teal. *Life and Death of the Salt Marsh*. New York: Audubon/Ballentine, 1969.

"A Terrible Tale from Dewee's Island." Charleston *News and Courier*, September 2, 1893.

Thacher, Davis. Diary of Davis Thacher, 1816–1818. South Caroliniana Library, Columbia, SC.

"Unendangered List." *Time*, May 18, 1998, 34.

Waller, Robert A. "The Civilian Conservation Corps and the Emergence of South Carolina's State Park System, 1933–1942." *The South Carolina Historical Magazine* 104, no. 2 (April 2003): 101–125.

Wayne, Arthur T. *Birds of South Carolina*. Charleston: Contributions from the Charleston Museum, 1910.

Wood, Virginia Steele. *Live Oaking: Southern Timber for Tall Ships*. Boston: Northeastern University Press, 1981.

Waddell, Gene. *Indians of the South Carolina Lowcountry 1562–1751*. Spartanburg, The Reprint Company Publishers, 1980.

Wright, Newell O., Jr. *A Cultural Resource Survey of the Cape Romain National Wildlife Refuge*. Valdosta State College: New World Research Reports 6, 1978.

Zarillo, Gary A., Larry G. Ward, and Miles O. Hayes. *An Illustrated History of Tidal Inlet Changes in South Carolina*. Charleston: South Carolina Sea Grant Consortium, 1985.

Maps, Charts and Plats

Bulls Island Quadrangle, Charleston County, South Carolina. Washington: U.S. Geological Survey, 1919. South Caroliniana Library, Columbia, SC.

Bull Island Quadrangle, Charleston County, South Carolina. Washington: U.S. Geological Survey, 1992.

Bull's Island. Plat. John Beresford, surveyor, 1697. South Carolina Historical Society, Charleston, SC.

Bulls Island, Jackson Creek—dividing line. Plat. Simons Mayrant, surveyor, 1907. Register of Mesne Conveyance, Charleston, SC.

Bulls Island (Site for Light House). Plat. B.B. Smith, surveyor, 1897. Register of Mesne Conveyance, Charleston, SC.

Casino Creek to Beaufort River, Intracoastal Waterway, South Carolina. Washington: NOAA, 1991.

A Plan of Bulls Island. Plat. Joseph Purcell, surveyor, 1793. Register of Mesne Conveyance, Charleston, SC.

Sewee Bay Quadrangle, Charleston County, South Carolina. Washington: U.S. Geological Survey, 1992.

Winyah Bay Entrance to Isle of Palms, South Carolina. Washington: NOAA, 1980.

Index

A

alligator 24, 31, 32, 42, 49, 50, 53, 72, 89, 99, 103, 111, 156, 176
American oystercatcher 73, 83, 129, 130, 139, 140, 144
Andersonville Mound 34, 110
Anderson Creek 21, 22, 29, 30, 36, 39, 40, 46, 49, 55, 59, 65, 69, 79, 87, 95, 104, 105, 110, 113, 119, 123, 125, 129, 135, 139, 145, 159, 164, 172, 175, 177
Audubon, John James 91
Awendaw Creek 110

B

Back Creek 152
barrier island migration 52
Beach Creek 164, 170
Beach Road 23, 31, 32, 33, 62, 89, 90, 122, 131, 134, 143, 153, 154, 155, 176
Beresford, John 22, 103, 123
Big Pond 33, 89, 156
Bird Island 49, 53, 55, 74, 80

bird migration 70, 82, 104
black-necked stilt 44, 63, 72
Boneyard 45, 50, 51, 52, 53, 54, 62, 63, 69, 72, 73, 100, 101, 111, 123, 124, 143, 144, 176
Bull, Stephen 41, 123
Bulls Bay 16, 17, 22, 39, 40, 41, 42, 49, 59, 79, 80, 81, 82, 83, 88, 100, 104, 110, 121, 159, 167, 169
Bull Creek 22, 30, 35, 36, 42, 88, 95, 100, 104, 119, 124, 125, 130, 131, 153, 159, 175, 177
Bull Harbor 22, 41, 102

C

Capers Island 61, 100, 101, 142, 165, 167
Cape Island 51, 52, 72, 82
Cape Romain National Wildlife Refuge 16, 22, 31, 40, 70, 71, 72, 81, 100, 112, 130, 140, 154
Carolina 40, 41, 44, 63, 114, 123
Carteret, Nicholas 41
colonial bird nesting 17, 74, 79, 80, 81, 82, 83, 84, 89
Cruikshank, Allan 122

D

deer 25, 89, 121, 143, 144
Dewees Creek 30
Dominick, Gayer 51, 154, 170
Dominick House 23, 33, 43, 88, 90, 94,
    121, 134, 141, 153, 154, 158, 170

E

endangered species 71
erosion 51, 52, 72

F

Fitzsimmons, Christopher 25, 94, 154
Five Fathom Creek 80, 145

G

Garris Landing 60, 99, 120, 164, 171,
    172
graveyard 17, 120, 122, 131, 132, 133,
    134, 167

H

horseshoe crab 69, 70, 143
Hurricane
    Fabian 109
    Hugo 33, 35, 36, 44, 51, 52, 53, 71,
        88, 90, 91, 94, 103, 109, 111, 121,
        134, 156, 168
    Isabel 109, 112
    of 1893 167
hurricane 51, 52, 168

I

Inlet
    Breach 61, 168
    Bull 22, 31, 40, 93, 102, 113
    Masonboro, NC 61, 63, 80
    Masons, NC 64, 101, 158
    Price 22, 31, 59, 61, 62, 99, 100, 101,
        102, 140, 142, 165, 167, 169
inlet
    dynamics 52, 53, 61

Intracoastal Waterway 16, 22, 25, 39,
    56, 59, 75, 83, 84, 99, 110, 125,
    149, 151, 159, 163, 165, 171

J

Jackson Creek. *See* Jacks Creek
Jacks Creek 40, 41, 42, 44, 72, 102,
    157, 176
    construction 50
John James Audubon 122

K

kingfisher 16, 87, 134, 139, 146, 149,
    150, 176

L

Lawson, John 44, 90, 91, 113, 121, 125
lighthouse 17, 53, 112, 154
Lighthouse Road 24, 53, 89, 123, 156,
    176
Little Bull's Island 60, 61, 100, 142,
    164, 165, 166, 167, 169, 170
live oak 89, 90, 91, 93, 134, 143, 153
live oaking industry 91, 92, 93, 94
loggerhead 15, 39, 41, 46, 50, 60, 65,
    71, 72, 73, 87, 121

M

Magwood 61, 83, 154, 166, 168, 169
    Andrew 165, 166, 167, 168, 169, 170
    Anna Butler 167
    Bessie Viola 132, 133, 167
    Bob 168
    Clarence 61, 165, 166, 167, 168, 169,
        170
    Earl 61, 62, 170
    Ethel 61, 62, 165, 166, 169
    James 132, 167
    James Elliott 167
    Junior 166
    Mary 61, 62
    Mildred 132, 133
    oyster factory 83
    Robert 167, 170

Mancke, Rudy 119, 120, 121, 122, 123, 124, 133, 156, 176
maritime forest 17, 23, 31, 32, 33, 34, 35, 42, 45, 52, 89, 90, 92, 94, 101, 124, 131, 134, 141, 143, 154, 155, 156, 165, 170
Marsh Island 69, 74, 79, 80, 81, 82, 83, 87, 121, 140
Masonboro Island, NC 63, 151
midden 33, 44, 112, 120
    Indian Kitchen Midden Mounds 34
Middens Trail 34, 35, 154, 158
Miller, Phineas 91, 92
Mill Road 31, 32, 33, 100, 101, 142, 155
Moore's Landing. *See* Garris Landing

N

National Recreation Trail 31
National Wildlife Refuge System 71
Native Americans 34, 40, 41, 44, 110, 112, 113, 141, 145
Navesink River, NJ 15, 70
New York Harbor 15
Northeast Point 22, 34, 35, 40, 45, 50, 51, 52, 54, 55, 59, 62, 63, 65, 69, 72, 87, 94, 100, 101, 104, 109, 110, 111, 112, 124, 140, 144

O

Ocracoke Island, NC 59
Old Fort 43, 141, 176
Old Fort Road 42, 44, 124, 140, 154, 158
Onisecaw 41, 123
Outer Banks, NC 42, 52, 59, 80

P

Pine Island Creek 152
Pregnall, Samuel 90, 167
Purcell, Joseph 22, 52, 152, 157

R

Raccoon Key 81
Romain Retreat 16, 21, 25, 26, 34, 50, 95, 103, 105, 149, 151, 154, 164, 171, 177

S

salt marsh 22, 52, 101, 102
Sandy Hook Bay, NJ 15
Santee River 22, 113
Sayle, William 41
Schooner Creek 62, 100, 142, 165, 166
seabeach amaranth 70, 71, 140, 144
sea turtles 73, 81
Sewees 41, 44, 113, 114, 141, 154, 155
SEWEE Association 119
Sewee Association 120
Sewee Bay 30, 41, 123, 153
Sewee Center 120, 133
Sewee Shell Ring 34
Shark Hole 30, 39, 49, 119, 130, 139, 159, 175, 177
Sheep Head Ridge Road 23, 156, 158
shrimp 103
    baiting 109, 111, 130
    trawling 62, 111, 142
Shubrick 154
    Edward Rutledge 93
    Irvine Templer 93
    John Templer 93
    Polly 157
    Thomas 52, 91, 93, 94, 157
    Thomas Sr. 23, 24
    William Branford 94
Spartina alterniflora 102, 103, 105
Summerhouse Creek 22, 35, 88, 95, 104, 120, 131, 135, 153, 159, 175
Summerhouse Pond 31, 33, 89, 122, 133, 134, 141, 154
Summerhouse Road 90, 120, 122, 131, 133, 134, 141

T

terns 54, 71, 73, 81, 82, 89
Thacher, Davis 25, 94, 102
turkeys 23, 35, 141
Turkey Walk Trail 32, 122, 133, 141

U

U.S. Fish and Wildlife Service 24, 51,
    71
Union invasion 110

V

Venning Creek 55, 74, 79, 83

W

West, Joseph 41
wolves, red 24, 71, 133, 170
Wrightsville Beach, NC 26, 61, 63, 80,
    151

About the Author

Bob Raynor is a longtime resident of Awendaw, South Carolina, which is situated along the Intracoastal Waterway directly across from Bull Island and Bulls Bay. A recreation therapist in psychiatry at the Medical University of South Carolina, Bob is an avid and accomplished sailor with over twenty years of experience sailing the waters off Bull Island. He and his wife Susan have two children.